VULGAR LATIN

JÓZSEF HERMAN

VULGAR LATIN

TRANSLATED BY ROGER WRIGHT

THE PENNSYLVANIA STATE UNIVERSITY PRESS
UNIVERSITY PARK, PENNSYLVANIA

Library of Congress Cataloging-in-Publication Data

Herman, József.
[Latin vulgaire. English]
Vulgar Latin / József Herman ; translated by Roger Wright.

  p.   cm.
    First published in France as "Le latin vulgaire," Paris, 1967.
    ISBN 0-271-02000-8 (cloth : alk. paper)
    ISBN 0-271-02001-6 (pbk. : alk. paper)
    1. Latin language, Vulgar. I. Wright, Roger. II. Title.
  PA2617.H413 2000
  477—dc21   99-35599
                                                                                                                              CIP

First published in France in 1967 as *Le latin vulgaire*. Copyright © 1975 Presses Universitaires de France

English translation based upon revised edition published by Editorial Ariel, S. A. Copyright © 1997

English translation Copyright © 2000 The Pennsylvania State University
All rights reserved
Printed in the United States of America
Published by The Pennsylvania State University Press,
University Park, PA 16802-1003

It is the policy of The Pennsylvania State University Press to use acid-free paper for the first printing of all clothbound books. Publications on uncoated stock satisfy the minimum requirements of American National Standard for Information Sciences—Permanence of Paper for Printed Library Materials, ANSI Z39.48–1992.

Contents

Prologue by the Author to the English Edition		vii
Foreword by the English Translator		ix
A Note on the Symbols Used		xi
Chronology of the Authors and Texts Mentioned		xiii
1	"Vulgar" Latin: Terminology and Problems	1
2	The Historical Context	9
3	Sources and Methods	17
4	Phonetic Evolution	27
	1. Vowels	27
	2. Consonants	38
	a) Word-Final Consonants	39
	b) Palatalization	42
	c) Intervocalic Consonants	45
	d) Consonant Clusters	47
5	Inflectional Morphology	49
	1. Nominal Morphology	49
	2. Verbal Morphology	68
6	Phrases and Sentences	81
	1. Noun Phrases	81
	2. The Simple Sentence	85
	3. Compound Sentences	87
7	Vocabulary	95
	1. Invariant Words	95

	2. Inflected Words	97
	a) Lexical Substitutions	97
	b) Semantic Changes	102
	c) Affixation and Compounding	104
	d) Foreign Words	105
8	More General Problems	109
	1. The End of the History of Latin	109
	2. The Geographical Diversification of Latin	115
	3. The Main Lines of Vulgar Development	120

Selective Bibliography   125

Prologue by the Author to the English Edition

The small book here being published in amplified and revised form first came out more than thirty years ago in French (Paris, 1967); it was reprinted unchanged later that same year, and then again in 1975. At the time, it was very well received, despite the modesty of its aims and the brevity required of books in the *Que sais-je?* collection, which suggests that it filled a widespread need in university courses. There were, of course, longer and more detailed handbooks on the topic, and this book had no intention of replacing those; but there was a place for a study that made it easier for all, specialists or not, to approach the unique phenomenon of the later history of Latin in the general perspective of language change.

When a Spanish edition came to be prepared for publication in 1997, however, it could not be merely a version of the French original. This was not because, or not only because, the text had a few technical flaws and was in need, here and there, of some rewording, but mainly because a translation of the original would not have taken account of the advances that had been made during the intervening decades in, for example, the field of historical sociolinguistics, or the general renewal of interest in Latin linguistics and grammar and in what has become an extremely active area, the field of Late and Vulgar Latin. On the other hand, I could not envisage writing a completely new book. I had neither the time nor, probably, the energy for that. Instead, I have made alterations in a number of details of greater or lesser significance, but have also left whole pages unchanged. The changes and additions have been made mostly in the chapter on the sources of Vulgar Latin, the chapter on morphology and syntax, and the final summary.

In this way I eventually prepared a French text that was, in effect, a new edition of the original, not just corrected and updated, but also completely revised and considerably enlarged. This text was then published in a Spanish translation (Barcelona: Ariel, 1997), thanks to the excellent work of Professor Carmen Arias Abellán, who also revised and expanded the Bibliography.

It was understandable, then, even inevitable, that the English translation should also be based on the revised and expanded version, which had already served as the basis for the Spanish edition. I should here like to express my gratitude to my colleague Roger Wright, who first took the initiative of arranging for its publication and then himself undertook the translation into English. He has done this with his usual skill. Not only has he managed to follow and preserve my train of thought, he has also carried out an admirable tour de force: the original French text, in its traditional formulas and syntactic complexity, followed an ancient Sorbonne tradition, from which I imagine I shall never be free, but under his pen it has been turned into clear English prose, easy to read, "user-friendly," which is always desirable in a work on linguistics. He also took the decision to work most of the original footnotes into the text and to adapt the Bibliography to suit the needs of Anglo-Saxon readers. I hope that the public newly reached by this book as a result of the English translation will receive it sympathetically and find it of interest.

J. Herman
Venice, March 1999

Foreword by the English Translator

Professor József Herman was recently heard to express a worry that he might have been misleading us into believing in the existence of something that in fact never existed; readers of this book will have to bear in mind continually that Vulgar Latin was never a language separate from Latin, but an integral part of that single complex system. "Vulgar Latin" has become a traditional term and has been defined in several different ways, not all of them compatible, so many scholars have preferred to avoid the phrase altogether. Professor Herman's definition of "Vulgar Latin" is certainly the best; it is just a collective label, available for use to refer to all those features of the Latin language that are known to have existed, from textual attestations and incontrovertible reconstructions, but that were not recommended by the grammarians. For that reason Professor Herman's comprehensive but succinct survey will be an invaluable research aid for all those with an interest in written Latin texts, and the speech of their authors, of the thousand-year period from Plautus to the late eighth-century reformers—that is, linguists, philologists, historians, literary critics, and many more. For this is not a minority interest: "Classical" Latin was spoken by almost nobody and written by only a few, whereas "Vulgar" Latin was spoken by millions of people over a period of a thousand years.

Professor Herman was for many years the Director of the Linguistic Research Institute at the Hungarian Academy and Professor of Romance Linguistics at the University of Budapest; more recently he has been Professor in the Department of "Antichità e Tradizione Classica" at the

University of Venice. He has become the master of this field. This is not just because he published the standard book on the topic in 1967 (of which the present volume is a revised and expanded version), and subsequently several other books and a long series of studies on these topics; not just because he founded and successfully encouraged the growth of the remarkably successful triennial international conferences on Late and Vulgar Latin; not just because he has been an inspiring friend and colleague to many who are attempting to understand this fascinating but complex topic; but mainly because, in a field beset by controversy, he remains a consistent beacon of tranquillity, perceptiveness, and common sense. Hitherto, however, he has only had published a few short articles in English. So it has been a real privilege to work on this translation, which we hope will make his merits entirely familiar also to the English-reading scholarly public.

I would also like to thank Christy McHale for preparing the excellent map.

R. Wright
Liverpool, April 1999

A Note on the Symbols Used

In this book, phonetic transcriptions are usually presented in the International Phonetic Alphabet (IPA), within square brackets. Forms in italics are the ordinary spellings of words. Thus [léwis] represents the pronunciation of the word spelled *levis*. Phonemes, speech sounds considered as functional units, often corresponding to the sound's mental image, are presented in their usual slash brackets, such as /o/. Some further symbols are traditional within the study of Vulgar Latin, and, where necessary, the following symbols have been used:

1. A small hook placed beneath a letter representing a mid vowel indicates that it is an open vowel, as in Vulgar Latin ę and ǫ. A dot placed beneath these letters indicates that it is a closed vowel, as in Vulgar Latin ẹ and ọ. Long vowels, however, are indicated with ":" in a phonetic transcription (e.g., [mi:sit]), rather than with the traditional macron, as in Latin *mīsit*; this has been done in order to avoid any possible confusion between written and spoken forms. An acute accent placed over a letter representing a vowel indicates that the vowel was stressed in speech, as in *vénio*. Semivowels are also transcribed as in the IPA; that is, the [w] symbol indicates the velar semivowel, as in English *win* ([wɪn]), and [j] indicates the palatal semivowel, as in English *yes* ([jes]).

2. The > sign indicates a direct etymological relationship; the open end of the > points to the Latin word, and the sharp end points to the Romance word or words that are the direct continuation of that Latin word. The words flanking the > are usually presented in their written form rather than in phonetic script, as in "Latin *gula* > French *gueule*."

3. An asterisk * before a form indicates that this form is not attested in writing at the time in question, although we have good reason to postulate its existence in speech at that time, in a phonetic shape corresponding to the spelling used. Thus *potere* implies that we wish to postulate the existence of an infinitive [potére] in Vulgar Latin (rather than, or perhaps as well as, the original infinitive form *posse*).

Chronology of the Authors and Texts Mentioned

(All dates are A.D. unless indicated as B.C.)

Ambrose:	4th cent.
Anthimus:	6th cent.
Antoninus of Placentia:	6th cent.
"Apicius":	4th cent.
Appendix Probi:	5th or 6th cent.(?)
Apuleius:	2nd cent.
Augustine:	4th cent.
Aulus Gellius:	2nd cent.
Benedict of Nursia:	6th cent.
Caelius Aurelianus:	5th cent.
Caesar:	100–44 B.C.
Caesarius of Arles:	6th cent.
Catullus:	1st cent. b.c.
Chanson de Roland:	11th cent.
Cicero:	106–43 B.C.
Claudius Terentianus:	2nd cent.
Commodian:	3rd cent.
Consentius:	5th cent.
Cyprian:	3rd cent.
Egeria (Aetheria):	4th cent.
Eulalia Sequence:	late 9th cent.
Faustus of Riez:	5th cent.

Fredegar:	7th cent.
Gaius Novius Eunus:	1st cent.
Gregory of Tours:	6th cent.
Historia Augusta:	4th cent.
Horace:	65–8 B.C.
Jerome:	4th cent.
Liber Pontificalis:	6th cent. onward
Livy:	59 B.C.–A.D. 17
Lucifer of Cagliari:	4th cent.
Marcellus Empiricus:	5th cent.
Mulomedicina Chironis:	4th cent.
Nemesianus:	3rd cent.
Palladius:	4th cent.
Petronius:	1st cent.
Plautus:	c. 254–184 B.C.
Pompeii Graffiti:	A.D. 79
Quintilian:	1st cent.
Sacerdos:	2nd cent.
Sergius:	5th cent.
Servius:	5th cent.
Strabo:	1st cent. B.C.–1st cent. A.D.
Strasbourg Oaths:	A.D. 842
Tertullian:	2nd–3rd cent.
Theodosius:	6th cent.
Varro:	116–27 B.C.
Vegetius:	4th cent.
Vergil:	70–19 B.C.
Vetus Latina:	3rd–4th cent.
Victor Vitensis:	5th cent.

1

"VULGAR" LATIN: TERMINOLOGY AND PROBLEMS

The phrase "Vulgar Latin" is regularly used in Latin and Romance philology and linguistics, although it is still one of the most controversial technical terms in these disciplines. As a result of the progress made by historical linguistics in the first half of the nineteenth century, however, the object of study called Vulgar Latin became unavoidable for researchers in the field. This came about in two ways.

It was, first of all, the result of a new discipline, the comparative study of Romance languages. The founder of Romance linguistics was Friedrich Diez; he was the scholar who raised the comparative grammatical study of the Romance languages to the level of a scientific discipline. The first edition of his "Grammar of the Romance Languages" (*Grammatik der romanischen Sprachen*) came out from 1836 to 1843. Some of the Renaissance scholars had had an inkling of these matters, but these nineteenth-century studies were the first to show incontrovertibly that the kind of language that must be taken to be the common origin for related words and similar phonetic and grammatical features in the Romance languages is often noticeably different from Classical Latin, as reflected in the works of Cicero or Virgil; yet this linguistic variety is Latin, even so. The following cases illustrate this (and they will be examined further during the discussion of the features they exemplify). As regards phonetics, for example, it turns out that the Romance languages sometimes have only one phoneme where it is clear that Classical Latin had two. This is the case with the Latin long /e:/ and short /i/, which, in syllables of the same type, always lead to a single result in all the Romance languages, except in Sardinia. Latin words such as *tela* and *credere* with long /e:/, and *pira* (plural of *pirum*) and *fidem* (accusative of *fides*) with short /i/, turn up with the same vowel in each separate area—in French as *toile*, *croire*, *poire*, and *foi*; in Italian as *tela*, *credere*, *pera*, and *fede*; in Spanish as *tela*, *creer*, *pera*, and *fe*; in Rumanian Latin *videt* with short /i/ became *vede*, and *credit* with long /e:/ became *crede*. There are large numbers of cases like this, and they show, among other things, that the linguistic variety from which the words in the Romance languages developed can only have had one phoneme rather than two different ones, the original short /i/ and long /e:/—from which we can conclude that this linguistic variety had phonetic characteristics different in some respects from those of Classical Latin.

As regards the vocabulary, there are many cases that allow us to come to similar conclusions. A great number of words in Classical Latin, perfectly ordinary words that were used to refer to straightforward everyday realities, do not survive in any Romance language. *Loquor* (speak) is a good example; this word has not survived anywhere in the Romance-speaking world, but was replaced by a variety of words that were at first comparatively peripheral and in some cases not even of Latin origin. Modern Italian *parlare*, Occitan and Catalan *parlar*, and French *parler* are words for "speak" that correspond to a Late Latin *parabolare*, formed from the Greek word *parabola*, which was characteristic in particular of Christian usage and came to mean not only "parable, analogy," but also "word," whereas Ibero-Romance, in Spanish *hablar* and Portuguese *falar*, and some of the dialects of Italy continue the word *fabulari*, which had existed in Latin all along but was less common than *loquor* and had the restricted meaning of "chat," the Logudorese dialect of Sardinia has a word for "speak" that derives from Latin *narrare*, and Rumanian has a word that comes from the Slavonic form *vorbă*, "word."

There are many such cases. *Pulcher* (beautiful) was replaced by other forms that were also ancient but less common and had slightly different original meanings, such as *bellus*, which led to Occitan *bel*, French *beau* and *bel*, Italian *bello*, and Rhaeto-Romance *bel*, *bal*, and *biel*; and *formosus*, which led to Spanish *hermoso*, Portuguese *formoso*, and Rumanian *frumos*. (Nouns and adjectives are usually quoted in this book in their nominative form, even though we know that most Romance nominals derived from the accusative; thus Spanish *hermoso* in fact came from *formosum*.) The Romance word for "fire" comes from Latin *focus*, meaning "hearth": Portuguese *fogo*, Spanish *fuego*, Catalan *foc*, Occitan *fuec*, French *feu*, Italian *fuoco*, Sardinian *fogu*, and Rumanian *foc*; but the Classical Latin word for fire was *ignis*, and this word has no continuation in any area of the Romance-speaking world. So in the field of vocabulary we must come to the same conclusion as we did in that of phonetics; the origin of the Romance languages lies in a kind of Latin in which, unlike in the Classical language, *loquor*, *ignis*, *pulcher*, and other words were used less than other words with approximately the same meaning, some of which even had foreign origin.

The philologists of the nineteenth century thus came to appreciate that Classical Latin was just one kind of Latin among many, and that the famous texts of the literary tradition disguise and conceal a linguistic reality that was very much more complex than that.

There were, however, data of another type, arrived at through other disciplines, that drew the attention of researchers to this kind of Latin. During the centuries that followed the Renaissance, Latin philology made great progress. Many late and medieval texts were studied and edited that had been unknown, or barely known, until then. In 1678 the French scholar Charles Du Fresne (Seigneur Du Cange) began to publish the huge *Glossarium Mediae et Infimae Latinitatis*, still not superseded, which included a large number of words and expressions that were not found in Classical Latin. Similarly, the old Latin inscriptions began to be listed and published, that is, the hundreds of thousands of Latin texts that were carved on stone or similar material all over the Roman Empire. The first published collections were variable in quality, but then the German philologists began the publication of the *Corpus Inscriptionum Latinarum*, bringing out the first volume in 1863, a work that is always being updated, even now. Other series of publications began in the first decades of the nineteenth century, such as the *Monumenta Germaniae Historica*, an enormous collection of texts from antiquity and the early Middle Ages that had previously been unedited, or hard to find, and that related directly or indirectly to the history of the Germans. Another example of such publications was the *Grammatici Latini* of Heinrich Keil.

Thus in the course of two centuries the number of Latin texts available for research increased significantly, and the quality and reliability of the editions improved noticeably, which meant that the published texts could be used for linguistic research. This wealth of available material from the post-Classical age, when exploited by philologists who had been trained in historical linguistics, revealed a wealth of linguistic data that did not match the traditional ideas concerning the grammatical structure of Latin. It thus became clear that the great majority of the non-Classical features in late texts, inscriptions, and other data from late antiquity and the early Middle Ages were not just "mistakes" and "barbarisms" but facts, and these facts needed to be understood as evidence of linguistic developments that did not correspond to the written Latin taught in the schools. And then gradually the scholars came to see that these textual details corresponded, in several essential respects, with the conception of Early Romance that could be arrived at by studying the languages that Latin was then turning into, even though these textual details led to a much more nuanced picture than the necessarily skeletal and schematic image produced by the comparative analysis of Romance. One example of these similarities (we shall see others later) was precisely the coalescence of originally long /e:/ and short /i/. We saw above that the Romance languages show that there must have been a stage of Latin in which what had once been two phonemes, short /i/ and long /e:/, became one; this evidence is corroborated directly in the study of the texts from late antiquity and the early Middle Ages, since in inscriptions from the later period of the Empire the letter *E*, which corresponded to the originally long /e:/, and the letter *I*, which corresponded to the originally short /i/, are confused all the time. We can find countless examples of this, such as the written forms *rigna* (for *regna*) and *minsis* (for *mensis*), or the other way round, *menus* (for *minus*) and *sene* (for *sine*).

This is how the idea arose of the existence of a non-Classical kind of Latin: as a result of the comparative analysis of the Romance languages and the late texts in the central years of the nineteenth century (although speculation on the topic had already occurred during the Renaissance and even earlier; this "prehistory" of "Vulgar Latin" research was first studied by Ettmayer: see the Bibliography). Since then the phrase used to refer to this kind of Latin has usually been "Vulgar Latin." This was an unfortunate choice, given the pejorative ring that the word "Vulgar" has in the ears of the layperson, but it had respectable precedents, for the phrase *vulgaris sermo* had been used by Cicero. Several scholars have been and are reluctant to use it, but the phrase has come to be a technical term now of long standing; it can hardly be avoided, in particular because the first large general study of this kind of Latin was called *Der Vokalismus des Vulgärlateins* (The Vowels of Vulgar Latin), and this authoritative work, by Hugo Schuchardt, led to the phrase's adoption in most of the handbooks that used Schuchardt's book as a source and a model.

And yet, in spite of the nineteenth-century discoveries that have just been briefly summarized, the notion of Vulgar Latin was still not very precise. It turned out not to be at all straightforward to work out satisfactorily the position of this Vulgar Latin within Latin as a whole, and it was equally difficult to develop a coherent theory that could explain the relationship between this Vulgar Latin and Latin in general. In a word, "Vulgar Latin" could not be easily defined. And that is still the case, over a century later; even now the precise definition of "Vulgar Latin" still forms the object of lengthy, complicated, and tedious discussions. There would be no point in going into great detail about all these controversies, so I shall merely summarize the main points at issue. The comparative scholars of the last part of the nineteenth century, especially Wilhelm Meyer-Lübke, one of the most important figures in the history of Romance linguistics, tended to see Vulgar Latin and literary Latin as two very different kinds of language, or even as two different languages altogether; as far as they were concerned, the written language was just an artificial disguise that was put over the living language of the people, which had been the "Mother Language" of the subsequent Romance languages; and this Mother Language could only be reconstructed, in their eyes, by the analytical comparison of its daughters. This way of looking at the matter survives in the work of some Romance historical linguists still, not always acknowledged, but is now out of date. Latin linguistics and philology made great strides in the twentieth century, particularly in the hands of Einar Löfstedt and his colleagues, and we can now operate with more precise ideas; instead of seeing Vulgar Latin to some extent as an imaginary "popular" Latin, we have become used in our research to collecting and analyzing the characteristics, features, tendencies, and developments that correspond to clear sociocultural criteria, to the spoken usage (insofar as we can reconstruct it) of Latin-speakers who were hardly, or not at all, influenced by educational and literary traditions.

We have also been working for several decades with more flexible criteria than those of the nineteenth-century scholars, since it is completely clear from the texts that during the time that Latin was still a living language, there never was an unbridgeable gap between the written and spoken languages, nor between the language of the social elites and that of the middle, lower, or disadvantaged groups of the same society. Of course, written Latin and spoken Latin were naturally different from each other, but that happens in every literate language; and despite the obvious rigidity of the Latin written tradition, the written language was continually being influenced by features of speech (to a greater or lesser extent, according to the educational level of the author, as well as the genre). This influence is most obvious in the many "Vulgar" usages that turn up in the later texts. But on the other hand, we should not deduce that Vulgar Latin is the same thing as spoken Latin merely because the object of study in the case of Vulgar Latin is in essence the spoken variety of Latin. Spoken Latin varied over time, certainly, but also according to the social class, the level of education, and the geographical and ethnic provenance of the speaker; there were undoubtedly in all the important cities groups of individuals, or whole layers of society, that tried to follow, even when speaking, the literary norms of grammar and standard vocabulary with care and respect (and greater or lesser success), while most Latin-speakers followed their natural linguistic instincts, whether or not these agreed with the traditional norms, even if they knew what these were. However, in texts prepared by uncultivated writers, who could hardly read and write at all, it was possible for innovations and "mistakes" to occur that would not necessarily turn up in their speech. Although the transition zones between these different kinds of language are gradual, not always perceptible at the time, there must have been such differences, just as there are obvious differences in Modern speech communities between the language, whether written or spoken, used by an educated person taking care to get details right and that of an uneducated fellow citizen.

Taking all these considerations into account, *in this book the term "Vulgar Latin"* (henceforth regularly used without these inverted commas) *is used to refer to the set of all those innovations and trends that turned up in the usage, particularly but not exclusively spoken, of the Latin-speaking population who were little or not at all influenced by school education and by literary models.*

This definition, though, still needs clarification, in three main ways.

1. This definition does not imply any chronological starting point. Since Vulgar Latin as so defined is in essence the spoken language of people who were scarcely influenced at all by the literary tradition, we can talk of the existence of Vulgar Latin only from the time when that literary tradition was first instituted, that is, at least from the last centuries of the Roman Republic. Even so, the first systematic evidence of Vulgar Latin that we have in any quantity comes from the first century A.D.: the inscriptions from Pompeii, the work of Petronius, and other texts discussed in Chapter 3. We do not normally use the phrase when investigating earlier times except when we are searching in older authors, in particular Plautus, for linguistic features that are infrequent or unknown in the language of the major Classical authors but turn up later. Anyhow, in the Classical age, in the last years of the Republic, for example, the linguistic distance between literary usage and everyday speech in Rome, even in the less educated classes of society, was stylistic in nature rather than based in any difference between linguistic systems. This is what Cicero says in his *Academica* (I.5): *non posse nos Amafini aut Rabiri similes esse, qui nulla arte adhibita de rebus . . . vulgari sermone disputant* (we should not be like Amafinius and Rabirius, who discuss the problems without any literary elaboration, in vulgar speech); here the term *vulgaris sermo* can be seen to mean "language with no rhetorical adornments." Indeed, in other places (such as his *De oratore* I.12) Cicero positively advocates the use of *vulgaris sermo*, whose intended meaning there seems to be "commonsense usage," without any pejorative connotation. As regards the chronological point at which the term "Vulgar Latin" ceases to be operative, that by definition coincides with the extinction of Latin as a spoken language (the dating of which is, inevitably, controversial: see section 8.1 below).

2. Since Vulgar Latin is by definition and in particular one of the spoken varieties of Latin, it should not be possible to talk of a "Vulgar text." The mere fact of writing necessarily involves the use of certain conventions based on the literary tradition or, at the very least, the standard orthography, even in the case of barely literate writers and whether they are aware of it or not. But it is possible, at least, to talk of a text as being more or less affected by the Vulgar variety, and it is in this sense that I shall use the expression "Vulgar text," however clumsy it seems, as a rough abbreviation for "a text markedly influenced by Vulgar usage."

3. It needs to be understood, when undertaking the study of Vulgar Latin, that this is a set of highly complex and ever moving phenomena; it naturally changed over time, and the usage of the first century A.D. was considerably different from that of the sixth century and later; it also varied from place to place, and these geographical differences vary in importance at different times. In addition, Vulgar Latin undoubtedly had stylistic subvariants within itself, such as the jargons used in different technical spheres; thus it seems certain, for example, that the Vulgar usage of the Christian communities was not the same, particularly in vocabulary, but quite possibly in grammatical details as well, as the soldiers' slang used in the same place at the same time. Under these circumstances, every generalization that is made about Vulgar Latin, without more precise reference to geography or chronology, is an abstraction. As such, it may be a justifiable working hypothesis, but it will be bound to cover up the surprising variety of the facts. Certainly, while evolving in constant interaction with all the other varieties, even the literary mode, to be found under the umbrella of Latin as a whole, Vulgar Latin had its identifiable trends and features. Even so, it is more reasonable to represent it as a moving and unstable kind of Latin than to try to construct a "Grammar of Vulgar Latin," which would be merely an illusion. As far as is possible in the brief framework of this present book, I shall try to avoid giving an oversimplified or unhelpfully abstract description of Vulgar Latin; and readers should do their best not to think of it as a static linguistic structure with clear and precise limits and well-defined, stable rules.

2

THE HISTORICAL CONTEXT

If Vulgar Latin has gained more importance in linguistic study than the "vulgar" varieties of other great literary languages, that is because of its extralinguistic historical context, which led to developments of great linguistic significance. The historical facts are well known in their general outline; they concern the gradual spread of Roman domination over the Italian peninsula and then over the whole Mediterranean basin. This carried with it the spread of the use of the Latin language, which was in the first place the language of Rome and the immediately surrounding areas, and then eventually, after several centuries, the first language used by almost everybody in Italy and most of the western provinces. This process needs careful examination, considering first the chronology of the expansion of Rome and then the immediate consequences of this expansion for the use of the Latin language.

The creation of the Roman Empire took over five hundred years. After more than two centuries of expansion, some of it military, some of it peaceful, Rome became the dominant power by the end of the third century B.C. on all the Italian peninsula and the large islands to the west of it—Sicily, Sardinia, and Corsica. In the second century B.C. the Romans conquered most of the Iberian Peninsula, the western part of the Balkans, Greece, and much of North Africa, Asia Minor, and the Near East. Toward the end of that century they took over the southern part of Gaul, the province called Gallia Narbonensis, and during the first century B.C. they extended their power over the rest of Gaul, Egypt, and the southern parts of what are now Switzerland and Austria. In the first century A.D. they came to Pannonia (essentially what is now western Hungary and much of Slovenia and Croatia), the western parts of North Africa, and Britain (that is, Britannia, approximately England and Wales). There followed some temporary gains on the eastern frontier, and then the emperor Trajan (A.D. 98–117) made the particularly important conquest, from the present point of view, of Dacia, which included a large area of what is now Rumania.

The linguistic Romanization of the conquered provinces was understandably a much slower process than their conquest, and in some places it was never completed. I should point out first of all, since this is of exceptional importance from the linguistic point of view, that Latinization nearly always happened because the population changed the language they used, rather than because of a change in the actual population itself. It is true that in several areas the conquest was accompanied by massacres, deportations of slaves, the capture of hostages, etc.; but except in a few cases where the military expeditions were explicitly punitive, the Romans generally respected most of their conquered populations. They had a long-term interest, after all, in the rational exploitation of the lands they conquered, and when the initial domination was assured, they made an effort to ensure that life was not too hard for their inhabitants. Thus in almost every province, particularly in the main ones round the Mediterranean, the native population remained the majority. So the linguistic Romanization of these provinces meant the gradual adoption of the Latin language by the native population. This adoption happened through contact with people who had come from Italy, such as soldiers, traders, colonists, and bureaucrats; it has to be conceded that the Romans did not adopt a conscious and direct policy of forcing their subject peoples to use Latin. The change to using Latin was thus the result of an apparently spontaneous process, of the pressure of many straightforward practical needs, and also, in many cases, of the cultural prestige that Latin had; but the changeover to Latin happened via several intermediate stages of both individual and general bilingualism, without any deliberate administrative intervention to that end from the Romans themselves. Under these circumstances we can understand why the Latinization of the provinces was a slow process, taking several centuries in almost every area; and also why it did not happen at all in the eastern provinces such as Egypt and Asia Minor. Here Greek was firmly in place before the Roman conquest, which meant that these areas already had available a language fully fitted for all practical communication needs and whose cultural prestige was far higher than that of Latin.

It is on the whole impossible for us to know exactly when the native languages stopped being spoken and Latin came into general use. The Romans themselves had almost no interest in the nature or fate of these languages, and anything they said about them is unhelpfully vague. Most were never or rarely written, so we have very few direct attestations of them. Those parts of Italy that were not originally Latin-speaking were naturally the first to be Romanized; and except in a few isolated regions, particularly in the mountains, cut off from the main roads and the large cities, Latin must already have been the language normally used all over the peninsula by the first century A.D. We know, for example, that in the small city of Pompeii, during the years before it was destroyed (that is, in the middle of the first century A.D.), Latin was the normal language, even though Pompeii itself lay within the Oscan region. On the other hand, it is worth mentioning that even in Italy languages of important civilizations showed a much greater resistance to the expansion of Latin than did the languages of the Peninsula whose speakers had no, or hardly any, written tradition; in the South, Greek continued to be spoken for centuries in some pockets (and perhaps continuously up to the present day in some isolated places), and it is possible that Etruscan, which indeed was the vehicle for an ancient cultural tradition, was still spoken in some places during the first centuries of the Empire. These chronological differences can be explained, at least in part, by directly linguistic factors: some of the languages, including Oscan and Umbrian, were closely related to Latin, much closer than Greek was (and far more than Etruscan was, which was not even Indo-European), so it is hardly surprising that those who spoke the more closely related languages such as Oscan and Umbrian (and others) found it easier to switch to Latin than those whose native language had deep structural differences from Latin.

In the other provinces of the Empire, linguistic Romanization was naturally slower. In Gaul it took at least five hundred years; the final extinction of Gaulish in the central and northern parts of Gaul probably occurred in the fourth or even the fifth century. It is also possible that Celtic survived unseen for several centuries in the Alpine valleys; the Britons, who began to come over to the Continent in the sixth century, may even have found in Brittany some groups who still knew Gaulish. In the South of Gaul, which had been conquered almost a whole century earlier than the rest and had received far more immigrants from Italy than the other areas of Gaul ever had, the originally Celtic populations would have adopted Latin much earlier. Some of the inhabitants of what is now Provence were, according to Strabo, Latin-speaking already by the last decade B.C.

As regards the Iberian Peninsula, there is still a great deal that we do not know. The Southeast of the peninsula was conquered long before Gaul was, and the province of Hispania had deeply Romanized cultural centers earlier than Gaul: Seneca, Lucan, Quintilian, and other writers came from the peninsula. But many tribes, belonging to several different language groups, had been there before the Romans came, and the penetration of Latin language and Roman civilization into the comparatively uncivilized areas of the North and West certainly took a long time. That the pre-Indo-European language Basque is still spoken in a wide area, on both sides of the Pyrenees, shows that the total Romanization of the peninsula was never complete.

In Britannia, a far-distant colony on the western edge of the Empire that held few attractions for the Romans, we can be almost sure that Latinization was confined to some of the cities and the areas around the military bases. Spoken Latin may not have survived long after the end of the Roman Empire here. But in contrast, the North African area was deeply Romanized, particularly in the Carthage region; there were still Latin-speaking populations here until after the end of the Vandal kingdom (in the sixth century), and they only died out entirely as a result of the Arab invasions of the late seventh century.

Romanization seems to have proceeded rather differently in the eastern European provinces (Pannonia, Dacia, Moesia), except along the Dalmatian coast, where the long survival of a Romance language that has only recently died out is proof of deep and stable Romanization.

(Dalmatian Romance was spoken throughout the Middle Ages in the coastal cities, and on the island of Veglia it lasted until the nineteenth century; the last native speaker died in 1898.) These areas were in general less developed and less heavily populated at the time of their conquest than those in the West, but they were of great military importance and thus had relatively more military garrisons and considerable immigration from Italy. This means that the spread of Latin could well have been quick; and yet the Romanized part of the population, less dense and less attached to the land than they were further west, were also less inclined to remain where they were at the time of the invasions from the North that began to sweep over these provinces in the late second century and returned with greater force in the third century. Toward the end of the Empire, the Romanized people of Pannonia were either destroyed or expelled southward toward Dalmatia and northern Italy, although there are traces of a few who perhaps survived for a while, for one or two centuries at the most, to the southwest of Lake Balaton. Dacia was abandoned in A.D. 270; possibly some groups of the Romanized population stayed there, although most of them withdrew to the banks of the lower Danube, in the province of Moesia. (The geographical location and the chronology of the development of Rumanian is still a controversial question and unfortunately confused by politics.)

In Germania and the Alpine provinces, Rhaetia and Noricum, the situation must have been similar to that in the regions of southeastern Europe; Romanization was not difficult, but it was superficial, due to a strong Roman military presence among some unsophisticated and relatively dispersed population groups. Later the Romanized element quickly weakened under the Germanic attacks, and only a few small Romanized areas survived in some isolated areas.

This was the route of the spread of Latin. What, then, were the consequences for the Latin language of this expansion? A detailed answer to this question is part of the description of Vulgar Latin and will thus be pursued at length in later chapters; for the moment, I shall be content to point out the main facts.

We can be sure that this progressive extension of the Latin language into populations that had not met it before created special circumstances, from the point of view of linguistic evolution. What generally happens in a linguistic community is that the language is transmitted from generation to generation, to "native speakers," that is, speakers who have that language as their mother tongue, whereas the integration into a linguistic community of other people, those born into other communities with different native tongues, only happens from time to time. But this case was different, since the arrival of speakers of another language into the speech community was happening on a large scale and all the time; the inhabitants of the provinces that were being Romanized in their own countries, and the slaves that were taken forcibly from their homes and transported to Italy, were continually being integrated into the wider Latin speech community, and formed, within that speech community, groups of foreigners who, at some times and in some places, outnumbered the native Latin-speakers. Bilingual people, those who can use two languages systematically and regularly, are usually an uninfluential minority in a speech community, but in the wide Latin-speaking community bilinguals must have been untypically common; the linguistic Romanization of the provinces undoubtedly occurred over a long period of bilingualism, which could even have lasted for centuries. When I return to consider the main trends of the development of Vulgar Latin at the end of this book, I shall be able to offer some kind of conclusion about the influence that these unusual conditions had on the development of the linguistic structures of Latin. It should also be said, though, in connection with bilingualism, that its growth in areas where Latin was the main medium of communication is not the only sociolinguistic factor that we have to take into account; the Roman Empire brought with it a wide number of other social changes, and all the time the distance was probably growing between the small elite who maintained as best they could the literary and linguistic traditions of the past and the larger sections of society who neither knew nor cared about these traditions; this too probably helped to accelerate the changes that were under way in spoken language, reinforcing the special features of what we call Vulgar Latin. I should also point out here that these external factors, historical, social, and sociolinguistic, are not the only, or even the most important, factors in the evolution of Vulgar and Late Latin. The interactions between internal linguistic factors, inherent in the structure of the language itself, and external ones, the social circumstances of the speakers and the conditions of language use, form a complex problem for the analyst, and I shall return to this theme in the last chapter of this book.

The spread of Latin over a very wide area, and the gradual adoption of Latin by very different groups of people with different ethnic and linguistic backgrounds, together with the different rates and depths of the spread of Latin, created the possibility that Latin would develop in different ways in different places. But this too is a controversial subject, which I shall return to at the end of this book, since only a detailed examination of the evidence can tell us how and when the geographical differentiation of Latin began.

Map

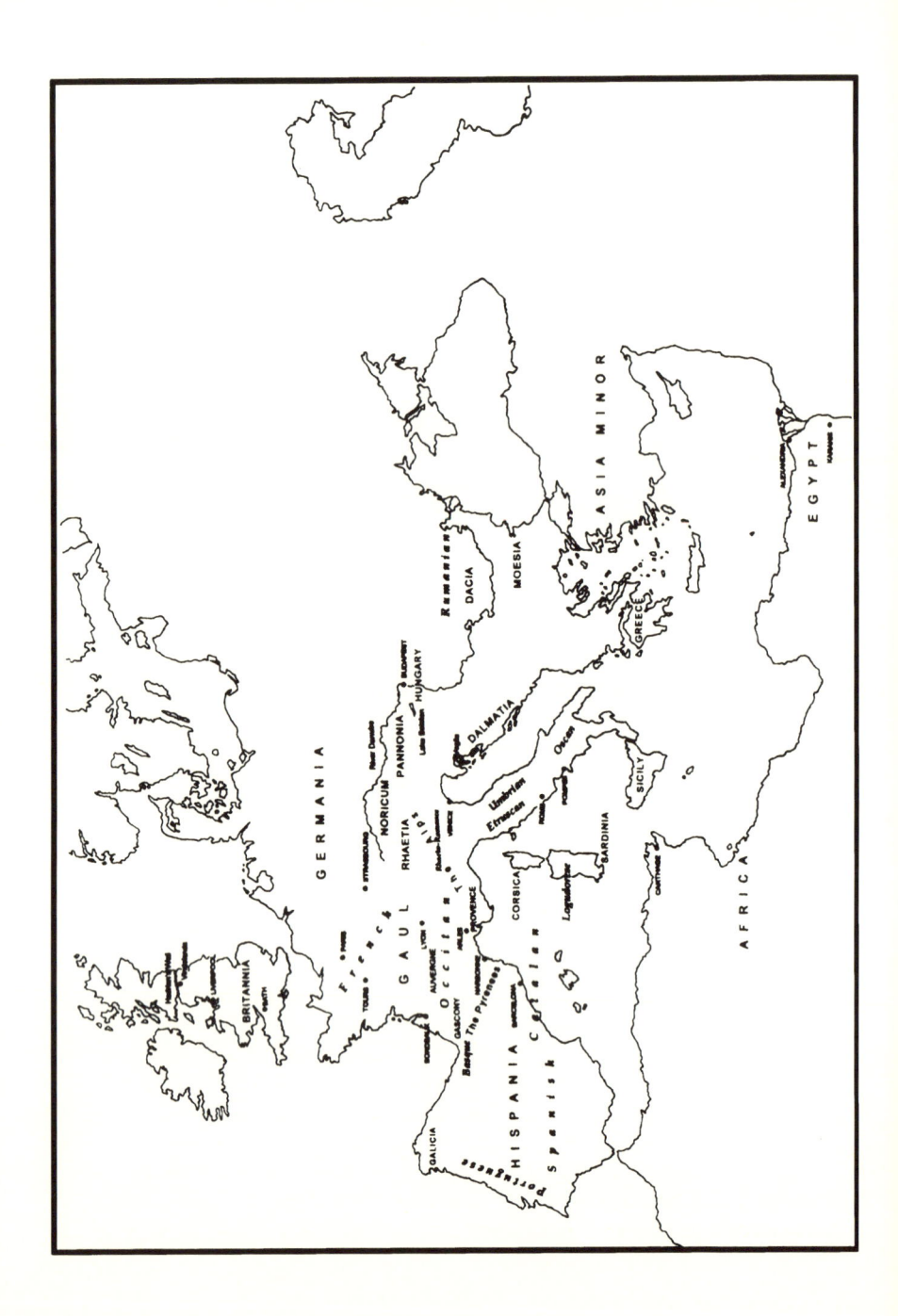

Regions and places labeled on the map:

- BRITANNIA
- GERMANIA
- GAUL (French, Occitan, Provence, Alsace, Lyon, Tours, Bordeaux, Gascony, Basque, The Pyrenees)
- HISPANIA (Spanish Castilian, Portuguese, Galicia, Barcelona)
- Languedoc
- CORSICA
- SARDINIA
- SICILY
- RHAETIA
- NORICUM
- PANNONIA (Hungary, Budapest, Lake Balaton)
- DALMATIA
- Etruscan, Umbrian, Oscan, Rome
- DACIA (Romanian)
- MOESIA
- GREECE
- ASIA MINOR
- EGYPT (Alexandria)
- AFRICA
- River Danube

3

SOURCES AND METHODS

Vulgar Latin is in essence a spoken variety of the Latin language, which means that there is no source that can allow us to grasp it directly. It is not at all common for Latin authors to make a conscious effort to reproduce everyday spoken language in writing, and when they do—as in Cicero's private letters, or some parts of the *Satires* of Horace—they represent, in a slightly edited form, the colloquial language of their own social group, that of the Roman intellectuals, rather than any particularly "vulgar" kind of language. Only one of the authors of the works that have survived, Petronius, in his *Satyricon*, deliberately tried to represent the natural speech of uneducated speakers, in the conversation of the guests at the grotesque Feast of Trimalchio. This contains some caricature and stylization, as every literary work does, but even so we have here a probably accurate sample of what the speech of slaves and freedmen could have been all over Italy in the second half of the first century A.D. This is, however, an isolated instance among the texts that have survived.

What more usually happens is that the texts that attest details of Vulgar Latin do so unintentionally. They reproduce nonstandard features because of the incompetence or casualness of their authors or copyists. The characteristic features of spoken Latin can thus be reconstructed on the basis of errors and inaccuracies in texts whose original authors probably aimed to write in an accurate or even literary style. When considering the most important kinds of texts, examples will be given of this "Grammar of Errors"; but this is not a straightforward matter, since we need to be able to distinguish the mistakes that really are due to speech habits from those mistakes and confusions caused by misreading letters, by the technical conditions of the production and preservation of the texts, or by mere accidents.

It is sensible to make a distinction between two kinds of texts that can give us information about Vulgar Latin: one group can be called "direct sources," whose linguistic features in themselves allow us to reconstruct details of speech; the others can be called "indirect sources," which are the comments or presumptions made by the contemporary writers who explicitly criticize a common "mistake" and thereby, whether they intend to or not, tell us about the way that the speech of the uneducated was tending to develop.

I shall begin by looking at the direct sources, which are altogether the most important. One main group of these comprises texts that have survived without any change in the form they had originally in antiquity, and have thus managed to continue to attest one or more linguistic features, as well as their original written shape.

1. Inscriptions: texts that were engraved or traced or at times painted onto hard and relatively long-lasting surfaces, and in particular those that are known as private inscriptions, such as epitaphs and individual votive offerings, offer valuable linguistic evidence. Even the inscriptions that were made in professional workshops were often prepared and engraved by craftsmen or workmen of no great education. Later, from the fourth to the sixth centuries, many of them, and especially the Christian ones, were carved by people who could hardly write at all. As a result, it is understandable that they would include mistakes that tell us something about speech. They have the further advantage of being located geographically and of having a date assigned to them, sometimes quite precise, sometimes within a margin acceptable to the linguist, and of forming, in total, a huge group of data; thus collectively they offer a wide gamut of possibilities for statistical research, since the number of inscriptions that have survived in the main imperial provinces

runs into the tens of thousands. It is also true that these advantages are balanced by drawbacks: they are on the whole very limited in their range of vocabulary and syntactic constructions and, in the case of the epitaphs, inevitably repeat over and over the same traditional patterns and formulas. In addition, it is normal for inscriptions, intended naturally to last and to be read for a long time into the future, not to be drawn up in normal spoken usage. This means that the conclusions of their linguistic analysis are not going to be equally valid at every level of the linguistic system.

Even so, we have available one large collection that can give us a varied picture, in the inscriptions drawn or painted on the walls of Pompeii, which, by a happy chance (for the linguist), have been preserved in their thousands by the ashes from the eruption of Vesuvius in A.D. 79; these can be taken to reflect more normal linguistic usage. The most complete published collection of Latin inscriptions is the multi-volume *Corpus Inscriptionum Latinarum* (abbreviated as *CIL*), which brings together, arranged by provinces and regions, all the inscriptions that were known at the time of its publication. (Because many of these volumes were first produced in the late nineteenth century, several complementary volumes have appeared since; some of these are in the bibliography at the end.)

When discussing the details of Vulgar Latin, I shall often adduce the evidence of inscriptions to illustrate a point; but first I shall here present a number of examples, partly to show what interesting data they are in themselves, but also to illustrate the awkward problems that can arise, and the mistakes that can be made, when we analyze them. For example, when we read in an inscription from the Lyon area in France the form *sene*, as opposed to *sine*, "without," we are looking at a common and characteristic mistake; since short /i/ and long /e:/ were not distinguished in pronunciation, we often find a letter *e* where we would expect a letter *i*. Another example of the same phenomenon can be found in the form *karessemo* (for *carissimo*) in *CIL* II 2997, from Spain; and there are very many others. Spelling mistakes of this kind—and the similar ones that confuse *o* and *u*—are motivated by phonetic details and are so common in every area of the Empire that a statistical analysis of their distribution and relative density can lead us to draw further linguistic conclusions (see section 8.2 below). Some cases are, of course, more complicated. For example, the words *memoriae Primitiui filio* (CIL XIII 3381), which have to be understood as meaning *memoriae Primitiui filii*, "in memory of their son Primitivus," can be interpreted as an example of the growing confusion, found in many areas, between the genitive and the dative case (see section 5.1 below). We can find the converse in CIL XIII 3816, *patris titulum posuerunt*, with genitive *patris* where we would expect dative *patri*, "they set up this epitaph for their father." But examples of this kind of confusion need to be considered individually, in detail, and with care, since it is often uncertain how the texts should be understood (and in fact this also applies to the two examples quoted here).

The next example shows how we need to take care in a number of respects even when it looks like a straightforward case. In Belgium, the northern part of Gaul, we find the form *coiuc* for *coniugi* (CIL XIII 3620) in a rather early inscription, probably of the second century A.D. The absence of the final letter is probably intentional, to save space (as often happens), so there are two details that need further explanation: the loss of the letter n and the use of the letter c rather than g. As regards the n, we should bear in mind that forms such as *coiugi*, *coiux*, etc., are normal in inscriptions; and we know anyway that an /n/ before /i/ or /e/ originally followed by a hiatus tends to weaken and even disappear in some areas, as happened to *uinea* in Rumanian *vie*, where the /n/ disappeared before the semivocalic glide that originated in /e/ before a vowel. All this could lead us to deduce that our inscription, lacking the letter n, is an unintentional reflection of the pronunciation of the author, unaware of the correct spelling. But this phonetic explanation is not the only one. We also know that the verbal prefix *con-*, as used in *consequor*, *consumo*, etc., often took the shorter form *co-* before a letter representing a vowel, or the letter *h*, as in *coerceo* and *cohaereo*; so the variation between *coniugi* and *coiugi* could merely be due to this alternation in the form of the prefix. On the other hand, the fact that here we find a letter c instead of a g is not of linguistic significance; the letters C and G, which had not been differentiated at all in the oldest Latin alphabet, were very similar, and it is not surprising that the man who engraved this inscription, who could well have been illiterate and clumsy, should have confused the two.

2. There are a number of texts that some scholars classify with the inscriptions but that are really a special group, with particular interest

for the linguist from the point of view of their purpose and their technical characteristics: these are the curse tablets, the *defixionum tabellae*, small sheets of metal, usually lead, used in magic and imprecations. They had written on them curses aimed at a particular person, which the gods in the underworld were asked to carry out. For this reason the tablets were buried in tombs. Writings of this type, in both Greek and Latin, are found in all the Roman provinces; in Britain several have been found in Bath, but the largest numbers of these tablets in Latin are found in Africa. In Audollent's collection of these tablets, no. 222, of the late second or third century A.D., includes the following imprecation: *inimicorum meorum linguas aduersus me ommutescant* (may the tongues of my enemies who speak against me be silenced); there are morphological details here of considerable importance, the use in *linguas* of the ending *-as*, rather than *-ae*, as the nominative plural of a noun whose singular ends in *-a* (see section 5.1. below), and the use in *ommutescant* of the spelling *-mm-*, probably representing [mm], the assimilated variant of what was originally [bm] and spelled *-bm-* (*obmutescant*).

3. Among the texts that have survived in their original form, a third category of documents derives from a real-life context: private letters, documents that record financial or business transactions, lists, school exercises, etc. Surviving texts of this kind are less common now than inscriptions are, since they were written on less permanent material, most notably papyrus. Papyrus is a writing material made by reducing the stalks of the aquatic plant of the same name to thin narrow strips and then joining these strips together under pressure. These papyrus sheets were used all the time, not only in private contexts but also in the ubiquitous bureaucracies of the Empire, so there must once have been millions of them. Unfortunately, papyrus is biodegradable, and it degenerates when exposed to moisture, so only a few hundred Latin papyri have actually survived for us to examine, mostly from unusually dry areas such as Egypt; this is why the eastern deserts, where Greek was the written language, conserved for us tens of thousands of papyri in Greek. In this way the records of a certain Claudius Tiberianus have survived in Karanis, in particular the letters that he received from his soldier son, Claudius Terentianus, a lad of little education or intelligence. These letters, presumably dictated to somebody else, are precious evidence of the normal language of the early second century. The text

(and numbering) is here taken from Cavenaile's collection, which brings together in one volume all the Latin papyrus texts formerly published separately, often in places that are hard to find; and here, for example, we read in letter 254.21–23 that *factum est illi uenire Alexandrie con tirones et me reliquid con matrem meam* (it so happened that he came to Alexandria with the recruits and left me with my mother). We can see here, in *matrones* and *matrem meam*, that the accusative case after *cum* is used at this time and place, rather than the original ablative (see section 5.1), as is the impersonal construction *factum est* plus the infinitive to mean "it so happened that . . . ," which was going to become normal at later times and was perhaps adapted originally from Greek. We also see here the locative use of *Alexandrie* for "to Alexandria," and a number of spellings that can be taken to show uncertainty caused by phonetic developments.

This category of real-life documentation also includes other texts on different materials, such as wax tablets and wooden tablets or planks. We have some interesting business letters on such tablets, written in highly vacillating orthography during the first half of the first century A.D. by Gaius Novius Eunus, a freedman from Puteoli, in which he confirms that he owes certain amounts; we also have letters written on wood by soldiers and their families in second-century Britannia, at Vindolanda on Hadrian's Wall, and other documentation in this category that will be referred to when relevant.

A second kind of source is represented by those texts that have come down to us through a manuscript tradition, usually via medieval copies; these enable textual critics to reconstruct, usually with some uncertainty, a text that was essentially the same as the original. This is a large grouping that includes, speaking generally, almost all Latin literature, but there are some kinds of texts that have special value as sources of knowledge about Vulgar Latin.

1. Technical treatises, such as those on medicine, veterinary science, agriculture, and so on, are very often written in a language full of Vulgar features. It is easy to see why: the artisans and others involved in these trades were often people from the less educated strata of society, often freedmen or people of foreign descent, who had not normally been given the standard education syllabus of grammar and rhetoric. Consequently,

these works were aimed at readers unlikely to insist on grammatical correctness or stylistic elegance. It is no surprise that the manuals that were compiled and assembled on the basis of existing Greek texts attested a kind of language not very like the literary norm. Among the books on veterinary topics there stands out the collection called *Mulomedicina Chironis*, probably from the fourth century A.D., which is often quoted subsequently; indeed, a few years later a writer called Vegetius (who may or may not be the same Vegetius who wrote a famous handbook on military matters) compiled a treatise for veterinary practitioners in which he reproduced great chunks of this *Mulomedicina Chironis* in laboriously classicized form. Palladius, who wrote an important handbook on agriculture slightly later than the *Mulomedicina Chironis*, in turn dedicated a separate chapter to the *medicina pecorum*. There are also a number of medical treatises; the *De medicamentis liber* of Marcellus (Empiricus) of Bordeaux, probably a fifth-century doctor, is a very interesting work from the linguistic point of view, and so is a shorter work on diet written by a doctor of Greek origin, Anthimus, who worked in sixth-century Merovingian Gaul. We also have a cookery book, the *De re coquinaria*, ostensibly written by Apicius, a famous *bon viveur* of the time of Tiberius; but the text is of a later period than that, roughly contemporary with the *Mulomedicina Chironis*, and almost every line of it shows the influence of the spoken language. For example, when we read in chapter 181 *Lactis sextarium et aquae modicum mittes in caccabo novo* (Put a measure of milk in a new bowl with a little water), we find, among other things, a wholly non-Classical use of *mittere* to mean "put" (it used to mean "send"), and also the use of the ablative rather than the accusative case in *in caccabo novo*, which reflects one aspect of the "vulgar" uncertainty in speech over the use of the accusative or the ablative case after *in* (see section 5.1 below).

2. Christian religious texts are also an important source for the study of Vulgar Latin. The earliest Christian communities were mostly from the least privileged parts of society, often not of Roman origin at all, and so the kind of Latin that the biblical texts were translated into—that is, those made before the great fourth-century translation of Saint Jerome, known as the Vulgate—had a popular character containing many nonstandard usages. For example, in one of the old African translations of the Book of Genesis (3.8) we see *absconderunt se Adam et*

mulier eius abante faciem domini ("the man and his wife hid themselves from the presence of the Lord," in the Revised Standard English version); subsequently, a version drawn up in Europe would change this text, turning *abante faciem* into *a facie*, and this adaptation was taken over by Saint Jerome into the Vulgate. We can see that the oldest text here used a combination of prepositions, *ab* + *ante*, to express a complex relationship (that is, *ab*, "movement away from," + *ante*, "position of one entity in front of another"); such combinations were not used in the Classical language, which is why the later European version, taken over by Saint Jerome, represents a return to the Classical usage. But such compound prepositions as *abante* must have been entirely normal in speech, since they are the origin of many of the prepositions now found in the Romance languages (in this case, *abante* > French *avant* and Italian *avanti*; there are other examples in section 7.1 below).

Of course, not all Christian texts are written in Vulgar language. Far from it; most of the Fathers of the Church were highly educated men, and some of them, such as Saint Augustine and Saint Jerome, had had a wide-ranging literary and even philological education, such that their own works were grammatically unimpeachable. Even so, as a generalization, it is fair to say that the linguistic characteristics of Christian texts as a whole, including those written in a literary style, are closer to those of speech than are those of contemporary texts of other kinds. There are several reasons for this. On the one hand, the Christian writers, even the best-educated ones, were following a specifically Christian stylistic tradition that had begun with the earliest versions of the Bible itself, which were characterized to some extent by features of spoken syntax and vocabulary, as well as by several features imitative of Greek; and in addition, several writers, including Saint Augustine, were deliberately trying to write in a style that was not too far removed from that of the normal speech of their congregations, particularly when compiling sermons and similar material, so as to reach the widest audience they could.

It is also true that some of the Christian writers of the first few centuries A.D. had had little grammatical or literary training. The texts of these writers are a mine of information about Vulgar Latin. This is the case with the anonymous authors of certain works that were once mistakenly attributed to Cyprian, and with the late fourth-century Christian

Egeria, or Aetheria, probably from Gallaecia (Modern Galicia) in northwest Spain, who compiled a diary of her pilgrimage to the Holy Land, of which, unfortunately, only parts survive.

Finally in this category come Christian funeral inscriptions, which are very different in their tone and phrasing from the pagan inscriptions mentioned above; they form a particularly useful corpus of attestations, since there are many of them, and they are all of a relatively late date (mostly later than the second half of the fourth century).

The classification of Vulgar texts just outlined is generally valid for the period before the end of the Roman Empire in the fifth century. But from the sixth century on, the lowering of general educational levels and the disappearance of the social layers that had continued Classical literary culture led to a decline in linguistic correctness in all types of texts and in every province that still spoke Latin. This decline happened to different degrees and at different speeds in different areas; it was particularly abrupt in Gaul, rather less so in Italy, and considerably less so in Visigothic Spain. This means that for works written in the centuries that followed the end of the Roman Empire, which is a crucially important time for the study of the transition from Latin into the various Romance languages, every text, in whatever genre, needs to be studied closely for the light it can shed on the development of spoken Latin at that time. In Merovingian Gaul, for example, such texts as the historical works of Gregory of Tours, the oldest versions of the Salic Law, the books of formulas used by officials when drawing up documents for private individuals, the diplomas issued by the Merovingian kings, and the saints' lives of the time are all useful material for the historical linguist.

The different kinds of texts that have been considered so far are the ones described as "direct" sources of information, and it is thanks to their linguistic features that we are able to establish the main features of spoken Vulgar Latin. But as mentioned before, we also have available indirect sources: writers of the time who mention linguistic matters and may thereby inform us about some of the details of the evolution of the speech of their time. The most useful of these remarks are naturally those made by writers with a particular interest in language and style. We have already mentioned some of the comments of Cicero (in Chapter 1); Augustine and Jerome and others have also given us important observations of this type, some of which are discussed later. We can also look at comments made by the Roman grammarians; when these are mentioning or criticizing a mistake that is commonly made at the time they are writing, they are giving us useful evidence on the development of speech. The grammarians' works are collected together in Keil's *Grammatici Latini* (abbreviated as GL); thus in GL, IV.517, when the fifth-century grammarian Sergius (whose name may just be a misspelling of Servius, who wrote famous commentaries on Virgil) tells us, *Nemo enim dicit de post forum, nemo enim ab ante* ("Nobody"—that is, nobody who speaks correctly—"says *de post forum*, and nobody says *ab ante*"), he is unintentionally attesting for us the existence of such compound prepositions in speech. Indeed, we saw an example of the second usage above. There also exists a kind of list of mistakes, the famous *Appendix Probi*, so called because, in the manuscript where it was found, it figures as one of the "appendixes," or supplements, of a treatise attributed to the grammarian Probus. This list, which may be of the fifth or sixth century, consists of a whole series of incorrect forms and misspellings, evidence of developments, particularly phonetic, that were probably common in the spoken Latin of the time and that were destined to be continued in the later Romance languages (there are examples in sections 7.2b and 7.2c below).

We have also already seen that some features of Vulgar Latin can be reconstructed by a comparative analysis of the Romance languages, as well as by the study of the actual Latin texts. In this sense these languages are in themselves an important source for the investigation of spoken Latin. The deductions that can be made from such a comparison of the Romance languages can only graduate from hypotheses to certainties when they agree with facts that have been accurately noted and checked in the texts; conversely, the evidence of the Romance languages is an essential control mechanism for distinguishing between those textual features that were caused by general long-lasting tendencies in the development of Latin and those innovations that were in comparison eccentric, accidental, or erudite.

4

PHONETIC EVOLUTION

1. Vowels

The Classical Latin of the Empire had what seems to have been a well-balanced vowel system. There were five basic vowels, each of which could either be long or short. Vowel quantity was phonologically distinctive; that is, the long and short pronunciation of the same vowel represented separate phonemes, which could thus be used to differentiate between separate words. Thus *malum* with short /a/ meant "bad," and *malum* with a long /a:/ was a different word meaning "apple"; *rosa* with a short /a/ was the nominative singular form of the word meaning "rose," and *rosa* with a long /a:/ the ablative singular form of the same word; *uiuis* with short [is] was the second-person singular of the present of the verb *uiuere*, meaning "you live," while *uiuis* with long [i:s] was both the dative and the ablative plural of the adjective *uiuus*, "alive"; *populus* with short /o/ meant "people," and *populus* with long /o:/ meant "poplar tree"; and so on in several other minimal pairs of words only differentiated by the length of a particular vowel. If we draw a diagram of the Classical Latin vowels according to their aperture (with the most open vowels—those pronounced with the lowest position of the tongue—at the bottom of the diagram and the most closed vowels—those pronounced with the highest position of the tongue—at the top) and the direction the tongue has to move in order to pronounce them (with the left of the diagram representing the movement of the tongue toward the hard palate in the front of the mouth, and the right of the diagram representing the movement of the tongue toward the soft palate in the back of the mouth), we construct the following vowel triangle:

/i:/   /u:/
/i/   /u/
   /e:/   /o:/
   /e/   /o/
       /a:/
       /a/

Latin also had diphthongs: *au*, as in *aurum*, "gold"; *ae*, as in *caelum*, "sky"; *oe*, as in *poena*, "pain"; and occasionally *eu*, as in *neu*, "nor."

During the first five hundred years A.D., and in particular in the two centuries preceding the end of the Empire, this system changed radically. On the one hand, the difference between a long and a short vowel gradually weakened, and the original phonological length distinctions, in syllables of all types, disappeared. There are various kinds of evidence for this. For one thing, the grammarians themselves tell us about it; in the late third century the grammarian Sacerdos mentions the tendency to shorten long vowels in the final syllable of words and calls it a "barbarism of our time," *barbarismus nostri temporis* (GL, VI.493–94). The confusion between long and short vowels seems thus to have begun in unstressed syllables, but it soon came to affect the stressed syllables too, and two centuries or so later the grammarian known as Sergius explicitly comments that "it is difficult to know which syllables are naturally long" (that is, which syllables contain a long vowel; *syllabas natura longas difficile est scire*, GL, IV.522).

The loss of these phonological distinctions of vowel length would probably have happened most rapidly in those areas where the language of the recently colonized population did not itself contain phonological length oppositions of this type; Saint Augustine, who lived in Africa, tells us in about A.D. 400, for example, that African ears do not make a distinction between long and short vowels (*Afrae aures de correptione uocalium uel productione non iudicant*, in his *De doctrina christiana* IV.10.24). It should perhaps be pointed out that this loss of the old phonological opposition between long and short vowels does not mean that all vowels came to be pronounced with the same length; what it means is that the surviving differences between longer and shorter vowels were no longer phonological, such that those differences could no longer be exploited by the language to distinguish between different lexical items. Length differences came to be directly determined by the nature of the syllables that the vowels were in; that is, they were now phonetic, secondary characteristics of vowels that were coming in Late Latin to be distinguished instead by different phonological features, as we shall see. When the fifth-century grammarian Consentius tells us that some people, and speakers from Africa in particular, pronounce the word *piper* (pepper) with a long vowel in the first syllable, when it ought to have been a short vowel (*quidam dicunt piper producta priore syllaba, cum sit breuis, quod uitium Afrorum familiare est*, GL, V.392), he is giving us just one of many examples of a stressed vowel in an open syllable (that is, a syllable ending with the vowel) that was tending to be pronounced longer than in the earlier Classical usage.

As well as the comments of grammarians, there are other indications that confusion over length had come into Vulgar Latin toward the end of the Empire. We can find mistakes in versification, for example, which get ever more common from the third century onward; the old metrical forms depended on the opposition between long and short vowels, and they come at this time to be used ever more clumsily. There are many examples; the Christian poet Commodian presents, to take just one among many similar examples, a hexameter ending with the words *datas a summo* (*Carmen apologeticum* 27). Here the first three vowels would in Classical Latin have been respectively short, long, and long, and yet the original hexameter meter required the line to end as $^{-\smile\smile}/^{-\breve{}}$; what has happened in this case is that Commodian reckoned that the first syllable of the word *datas*, which was the stressed one, must have technically been a long one, and that both the second syllable of that word and that of the atonic word *a* must have been short because they were not stressed.

The evidence of all the Romance languages is unanimous. It all shows that the old system of vocalic length fell into disuse. Long and short vowels have developed identically in Sardinia, for example in the Logudorese dialect, where *filum*, "thread," with a long /i:/, has developed the same way as *sitis*, "thirst," with a short /i/, into *filu* and *sidis* respectively. In most other Romance areas the originally long /i:/ remains as /i/, but the long /e:/ and the short /i/ have developed identically to become the same phoneme in the ensuing Romance language; the Spanish words for "thread" and "thirst" are *hilo* and *sed*, and the French words are *fil* and *soif*. In the Romance languages as a whole the length of time during which a vowel is pronounced is determined by other factors entirely, not related to whether the original Classical vowel had been long or short.

The loss of the length system (vowel quantity) seems to have been accompanied by a reorganization of how open or closed the vowels were (vowel quality). It seems certain that from the start long vowels were more closed (pronounced with a higher position of the tongue) than their short counterparts. Originally these differences in quality were secondary, not distinctive, but as time went on and the length distinctions decayed, they became essential distinctive features. Thus the words *uenit*, "comes," with a short /e/, and *uenit*, "came," with a long /e:/, were distinguished in the original Latin pronunciation by the fact that the two /e/s were quantitatively distinct; these two words indeed remained distinguishable in the later period, but the feature that made the words distinctive then was no longer their relative quantity; these two [e]s now had the same length (which was probably relatively long in this case, since the syllables concerned were stressed and open; that is, they ended in the vowel); the distinctive feature was by that time their relative quality, the same difference that had already existed in earlier times without being significant and was reinforced in this later time to become phonologically functional. The originally short vowel had become an open /ɛ/, and the originally long vowel had become a closed /e/, and as a result the pronunciation of "comes," *uenit*, could still be distinguished from that of "came," *uenit*. In the case of the /a/, which is the most open vowel of all, relative quality did not become distinctive in this way; the short /a/ and the long /a:/ merged into a single phoneme /a/. The open version of the /i/ and the open version of the

/u/, both originally short, did not survive as separate phonemes; in most places, originally short /i/ and originally long /e:/ merged into a single phoneme, the closed /e/, and in the same way, the back vowels originally short /u/ and originally long /o:/ merged into a single phoneme, the closed /o/; this was because in each case the mode of articulation of the two was similar, as was their sound.

The diphthongs also developed. *Eu* disappeared because the few words that had contained it fell out of general use. *Ae* and *oe*, however, became monophthongs at an early date, probably in the first century A.D.: *ae* became open /ɛ/, and *oe* became closed /e/. These changes are attested by countless spelling mistakes, in particular those that used the letter *e* instead of the letters *ae* in, for example, *filie* for *filiae*. The *au* diphthong, on the other hand, survived throughout, even though certain dialect areas saw it monophthongize as [o]; indeed it persists in some Romance areas, including not only Old Occitan but Modern Rumanian (e.g., Latin *aurum* > Rumanian *aur*, "gold"), and some other Modern dialects.

We can illustrate this reorganization of the vowels (as it applied to stressed syllables, at least) as follows:

Original Latin: a   a: e   e: i   i: o   o: u   u:

Vulgar Latin: a   ɛ   e   i   ɔ   o   u

(In the second line of this diagram, the traditional notation for ɛ, e, ɔ, and o would be ẹ, ẹ, ọ, and ọ). There is abundant evidence for this. There are many spelling confusions in the later inscriptions; I have already mentioned here the common use of the letter *i* for what would originally have been an *e*, representing a long /e:/, and conversely the use of the letter *e* in place of an *i* to represent what would originally have been a short /i/. For the speakers of the time, there was only one sound, represented in correct spelling sometimes by one of these letters and sometimes by the other, and the less well educated authors and engravers of the inscriptions were naturally often unsure which to use: we find, for example, the forms *rigna*, *tris*, and *minsis* instead of the correct forms *regna*, *tres*, and *mensis* ("reigns," "three," and "month"), in which the letter *e* originally represented a long /e:/; and conversely the forms *sene, vigenti*, and *claressimus* instead of the correct forms *sine, viginti*, and *clarissimus* ("without," "twenty," and "very notable"), where the letter i in question originally represented a short /i/. There are a similar number of confusions between the letters used to represent the back vowel /o/; such as *matrunae, honure*, and *territurium* instead of the correct forms *matronae, honore*, and *territorium* ("wife," "honor," and "territory"), where the letter o in question originally represented a long /o:/; and conversely the forms *nomero, tomolo*, and *sous* instead of the correct forms *numero, tumulo*, and *suus* ("number," "tomb," and "his own"), where the letter *u* in question originally represented a short /u/. These examples all come from inscriptions in Gaul, which has hundreds of such spellings to offer, but most of the regions of the Empire have similar phenomena, including Hispania, North Africa, and Italy; they occur mostly in later inscriptions, particularly the Christian ones.

The evidence of the subsequent Romance languages clearly shows, in most areas, that this Vulgar Latin vowel system did indeed once exist. Originally long /e:/ and originally short /i/ turn up as a single phoneme in the great majority of the Romance languages outside Sardinia (as we saw above and will see again), and the same is true of originally long /o:/ and originally short /u/; thus Latin *uotum*, "vow," which originally had a long /o:/, and Latin *gula*, "throat," which originally had a short /u/, turn up each with the same vowel as the other in each Romance area, even though the areas sometimes differ in the outcome; Spanish and Catalan have *boda* (through a semantic specialization of the plural *uota*, "marriage vows, marriage") and *gola*, Italian has *voto* and *gola*, and French has *voeu* and *gueule*.

This evidence from Romance gives us a chance to work out in which areas these changes did and did not occur; it suggests that this reorganization of vowel quality did not occur in Sardinia, and occurred only partly in the Latin spoken at the eastern end of the Empire. Vowel quality in Sardinia remained as it had been all along, even though the length distinctions were lost here as everywhere else; thus French *fleur* ("flower," < Latin *florem*, with an originally long /o:/) and *gueule* correspond to the forms, in the Logudorese dialect of Sardinia, *flore* and *bula*; while almost everywhere else these two vowels merged as one, Vulgar Latin /o/, they continued to be pronounced with differing vocalic quality in Sardinia as they had been in Latin. The same happened with the front vowels, as we saw above (with Sardinian *filu* and *sidis*). In Rumania, on the other hand, we find a development halfway between the two; the front vowels merge, as in most of Romance, but the difference in quality is preserved in the back vowels, as in Sardinia. Latin *florem* gives Rumanian *floare*, but Latin *gula* gives Rumanian *gură*, so that the distinction between the original Latin phonemes is still maintained.

Sicily shows us a different pattern again; here, in stressed syllables, all of originally long /iː/, originally short /i/, and originally long /eː/ have merged as the one phoneme /i/; and similarly, originally long /uː/, originally short /u/, and originally long /oː/ have merged as /u/. Thus in Sicily we find *crita* from Latin *creta* with a long /eː/ ("clay, chalk," as opposed to mainland Italian *creta*), and *niputi* from Latin *nepotem* with a long /oː/ ("grandson," as opposed to mainland Italian *nipote*). For this reason, some of the Romance linguists have argued that there exists a fourth variety of Vulgar Latin vowel system, the Sicilian variety; but we would do better to consider this as a secondary development of the main type.

If we draw up the Vulgar Latin vowel triangles along the lines we did for Classical Latin above, according to what happened in different areas, they thus look like this:

(*a*) In the West and the center of the Empire:

/i/ /u/
/ẹ/ /ọ/
/ę/ /ǫ/
/a/

(*b*) In the Balkans:

/i/ /u/
/ẹ/
/o/
/ę/
/a/

(*c*) In Sardinia:

/i/ /u/
/e/ /o/
/a/

The complete or partial survival of the original vocalic qualities, in Sardinia, Rumania, and some areas of the southern Italian mainland, can be thought of as an archaic feature; and it has sometimes been argued that these are peripheral regions, isolated since early times from most of the Romanized world, and that this is why they still reflect an early stage in the evolution of Vulgar Latin, in which the eventual regrouping of the vowels had not yet been completed. There could be some truth in this; in some areas, probably the majority, the reorganization of the front vowels, which did happen in Rumanian, seems to have happened before the reorganization of the back ones, which did not happen in Rumanian. There are, in fact, many territories, even in the West, where the inscriptions show signs of confusion in the back vowels later than in the front vowels. In Sardinia, the vowel system lost the phonological length distinctions but still kept the original vocalic qualities. This seems to imply that the reorganization of vocalic qualities, while appearing to be closely linked to the loss of the phonological length distinctions, occurred later than that and was only partially a consequence of it.

The changes we have been discussing apply to vowels in stressed syllables. Developments are not so clear in the unstressed vowels; in these the loss of the length distinctions happened before it did in the stressed vowels, and the confusion of vowel quality then went further than it did in the stressed vowels. For example, most of the Romance regions have /e/ in an unstressed final syllable coming from all of Latin long /e:/, short /e/, and short /i/. Thus in fifth-century epitaphs we are as likely to find written *iacit* as *iacet* (which is the correct form, "lies"), and *requiescet* as *requiescit* (which is the correct form, "rests"); the form *mensis*, for the correct accusative plural form *menses*, "months," is also common. In proparoxytone words (where the stressed syllable is the third from the end) the unstressed vowel in the penultimate syllable is particularly weak and liable to disappear entirely; there are early attestations of the form *caldus* for *calidus* (hot), and the use of *domnus* and *domna* rather than the correct *dominus* and *domina* ("lord" and "lady") is common in later inscriptions. These cases were only sporadic overall at that time, but later on large numbers of these unstressed penultimate vowels were due to disappear; for example, Latin *uiridem* (green) turns up as *verde* in Portuguese, Spanish, Italian, and Rumanian, *vert* in French and Occitan, and *birde* in Sardinian. Not all the languages were going to go equally far in this respect, however. Many of these proparoxytone Latin words still preserve their penultimate vowel in Rumania, Italy, and Sardinia, while further west they are far more likely to lose it than not (unless it is /a/): thus we have Latin *fráxinum* (ash tree) becoming Italian *frassino* and Rumanian *frasin*, but French *frêne*, Spanish *fresno*, and Catalan *freixe*.

Two other details concerning vowels should be mentioned briefly here. The first concerns the appearance of an initial letter *i*, or sometimes *e*, known as a prothetic vowel, at the start of words beginning with *s* and a consonant. Thus we find written *iscripta* for the correct *scripta* (writings) in many places, including Christian inscriptions in Rome itself. This phenomenon turns up all over Romance, but particularly in the West; thus the Latin verb *scribere* (write) has become Spanish *escribir*, Catalan *escriure*, and Portuguese *escrever*; it also became Old French *escrire*, now *écrire*. The second concerns the semivowel (or semiconsonant) transcribed in the International Phonetic Alphabet as [j] (the sound at the start of, e.g., English *yes*). This sound existed in Classical Latin, mainly at the start of a word (e.g., *iam*) or intervocalically (e.g., *maior*), but in Vulgar Latin the [j] came to be used in many more positions, in particular postconsonantally. This was because unstressed /e/ and /i/ came to be pronounced [j] immediately before another vowel. There is copious Romance evidence for this, but also confusion in written Latin about whether words containing the [j] should be written with *i* or *e*; thus a Christian inscription from Lyon in France (*CIL* XIII 11213) has the form *ueator*, rather than the correct *uiator* (a personal name, meaning "traveler"), and one from Dalmatia (*CIL* III 9503) has *niofita* for *neofita* (neophyte).

The phonetic developments that we have looked at so far show how important the position of the stress was. The difference in evolution between stressed and unstressed vowels, the tendency of stressed vowels to grow longer in an open syllable, and the weakness of several unstressed vowels demonstrate that the stress accent had an important role to play in the development of the vowel system, a role that probably expanded during the first few centuries A.D. It also seems likely that the nature of the stress itself changed after the Classical period. According to one theory, which used to be more widely held than it is now, the nature of the stress on Latin words during the Classical period was a tone accent (involving higher melodic pitch than on the other syllables) rather than a simple stress accent as in Romance (involving intensity, with the stressed syllable being pronounced louder than the others); then, according to this theory, during the evolution of the post-Classical language, a stress accent replaced the tone accent. This theory was largely based on the comments of the grammarians, who all mention a melodic accent in the earlier times (on the analogy of Greek, which indeed had such an accent) and only talk about relative loudness from the fourth century. The arrival of a rhythmic kind of verse toward the end of the Empire also suggests that there could have been a change in the nature of the accent. But these arguments are not hard to argue against; some phonetic data indicate that the accentuation of archaic (pre-Classical) Latin also involved intensity, suggesting that such an accent had been there all along.

Both hypotheses—that the stress accent had emerged in post-Classical times, and that it had merely been reinforced then—seem sufficient to explain the relevant details of the evolution of spoken vowels. A strong stress accent, which concentrates the articulatory energy on the stressed syllable, can in itself lead to the relative weakening of the unstressed syllables; in the same way, by encouraging the lengthening of a stressed short syllable, a reinforced stress accent could lead to the weakening of the original phonological oppositions between long and short vowels. This could even have been the factor that triggered the changes. Following this line of thought we can come up with an apparently coherent chain of cause and effect, in which the tendency to reinforce the existing stress accent (or its appearance in the first place, if we still think there was only a tone accent in the Classical period) would thus be the cause responsible for all the main changes that then took place in the spoken vowel system. But unfortunately it would be as well to remain a bit skeptical about this; some languages, such as Hungarian, for example, have a very strong stress accent involving intensity and at the same time a whole operating phonological system of vowels based on distinctions of length, so clearly a strong stress accent and a vowel system based on phonological length distinctions are not necessarily in themselves incompatible. If indeed these two phenomena became incompatible in post-Classical Latin, that must have been due, in addition, to other factors peculiar to Latin that have not yet been adequately understood.

In addition to these explanations that tie the stress accent to the development of the phonology of the vowels, explanations of a different kind have been put forward to explain what happened. Experts in historical phonetics have suggested that these developments might have had an internal structural motivation within the system itself. André Haudricourt and Alphonse Juilland (in 1943) suggested that the system needed a "restructuring" after the disturbances caused to it by the monophthongization of the original diphthongs; and Harald Weinrich (in 1958) proposed an argument based on the possibility that there were imbalances in syllabic structure. I myself, looking at relevant statistics and having recourse to some aspects of information theory, have thought that the motivation for these changes could lie in the inequalities of the functional load that existed between the different phonological vowel oppositions (see my 1990 collection, 196–203). There have been yet other suggestions; and overall we can conclude that the theoretical problems connected to this most important development, the reorganization of the vowel system in Late Latin, have not yet been solved to general satisfaction.

It is worth adding that although the nature of the accent was either changed (from melodic to stress) or modified (reinforcing the stress), its position in the word hardly ever changed. The syllable that carried the accent in a Classical Latin word also carried it in Vulgar Latin, and usually that is still the syllable that is stressed in the Romance word too; for example, Latin *ciuitátem* (city) has become *cité* in France, *città* in Italy, *cetáte* in Rumania, *cidade* in Portugal, and *ciudad* in Spain, all with a stressed [á] (now represented with *é* in the French word); Latin *púluerem* (dust) has become *poudre* in France, *pólvere* in Italy, *púlbere* in Rumania. There are only two kinds of words, neither of them numerous, in which the Vulgar Latin stress seems to have changed from one syllable to another. Unstressed penultimate vowels followed by a plosive consonant plus [r] acquired the stress in speech, and it is still there in Romance; for example, the original Latin *ténebrae* (shadows) was *tenébrae* in Vulgar Latin, and the penultimate is still the stressed syllable in Spanish *tinieblas*; the French word *ténèbres* is a later erudite borrowing from Latin. Furthermore, a stressed [é] or [í] followed by another vowel lost the stress to that following vowel; for example, the original Latin *filíolum* (small son) was *filiólum* in Vulgar Latin, and that is still the stressed syllable in French *filleul* and Spanish *hijuelo*.

2. Consonants

As far as the vowels are concerned, almost all the evidence from Romance allows us to reconstruct a Vulgar Latin system that was for the most part common to all areas, a system that implies a general change from the original. The consonants of Vulgar Latin, however, suffered only a few isolated and peripheral developments early enough for them to be reflected all over the Romance world. The main systematic reorganizations of the consonants happened comparatively late and were not the same in all Romance regions.

First we can mention a change that happened in the Republican period, that is, even before the Empire; the laryngeal aspirate /h/ was dropped, in all positions in a word. Many spelling errors demonstrate this; inscriptions very often drop a letter *h* where correct orthography required one, as, for example, *ic* for *hic* (here), and *abere* for *habere* (have). Conversely, there are hypercorrections with an unnecessary letter *h*, such as the form *holim* for *olim* (once). This situation became confused for a while, however, by the arrival into the Latin vocabulary of many Greek words that had laryngeal aspirates and aspirated consonants of the kind regularly written with the letters *th*, *ch*, and *ph*; and it seems likely that the linguistic pretentiousness of some Romans who knew the Greek pronunciation actually led them to attempt to pronounce such words in a Greek way, with [h] sounds all over the place, even in cases where the words were not actually Greek at all. In a famous epigram (no. 84) Catullus makes fun of this way of talking, characterizing someone called Arrius as so high-faluting that he said *hinsidias* for *insidias*, and *chommoda* for *commoda*. But this was a sporadic and passing phase, which had no consequences for the subsequent development of the sounds, and no trace of [h] survives in Romance speech.

Another general change that happened comparatively early affected the [w] in nonvocalic position, written with the letter *u*, in words such as *grauis* (heavy) and *uiuere* (to live), which in this book I spell with *u* (although often they are now printed with a *v*, as *gravis* and *vivere*). This was originally a labiovelar semivowel in which the movement of the lips coincided with a marked raising of the back of the tongue toward the velar palate. The sound was thus at that time different from the labiodental [v] found in most Romance languages, such as French *vivre* and Italian *vivere*, and also from the voiced bilabial fricative sound [β], represented by the second letter *v* in Modern Castilian Spanish *vivir*. But the velar part of this sound was soon lost, perhaps around the end of the Republican period, and the sound became the voiced bilabial fricative (the one that still survives in Spanish). The main evidence for this lies in the very common spelling mistake that confused the letter *u*, which represented the semivowel in words of this type, with the letter *b*, which represented the normal voiced bilabial plosive [β]; this latter phoneme was suffering a weakening process anyway in certain positions in the word, becoming increasingly fricative (see section 4.2c below). In most of the Romance world, this bilabial fricative [β] then became, during the first few centuries A.D., the labiodental fricative [v]. There is epigraphic evidence for this latter development, too; the substitution of the letter *n*, which represents the dental nasal [n], for the letter *m*, which represents the bilabial nasal [m], in forms such as *decenuir* rather than the correct *decemuir* (magistrate), and *eunue* rather than *eumue* (or him), shows that the nasal consonant has assimilated to [n] in order to be homorganic with a following labiodental [v], rather than with the original bilabial [b].

These two consonantal changes, affecting [h] and [w], happened independently of their position in the word. The other consonantal changes only occurred in some phonetic contexts, depending on the position of the consonant in the word or even in the phrase.

a) Word-Final Consonants

At the end of a word, final [m] already seems not to have been pronounced by the first century B.C. When a word with an *-m* at the end appeared before a word beginning with a vowel in verse, the word was treated as ending in a vowel, so the presence of the -m did not prevent the normal contraction of the two vowels into a single syllable for metrical purposes. Thus in Virgil's *Aeneid*, iv.129, we read *Oceanum interea surgens Aurora reliquit*; here the first two words have to scan as ¯ ˘ ˘ / ¯ ˘ ˘ / ¯, which implies that the -*num* and the *in*- together form just one syllable. In the first century A.D., Quintilian states that the final /m/ before a vowel was hardly perceptible, and it seems likely that from then on final /m/ survived, if at all, just as a nasalization of the previous vowel, particularly if the next word began with a vowel. Words in inscriptions were sometimes written without final *m* from the earliest times, and in the later inscriptions the omission is ubiquitous. As representative examples, chosen more or less at random and from different areas, we could quote *dece* for *decem* (ten), and *contra uotu* for *contra uotum* (against the vow). (As pointed out in the previous chapter, though, we need to be aware of cases where such an omission might be due to rather more practical considerations, such as lack of space at the end of a line; the examples quoted from inscriptions here are all chosen from cases where these cannot apply.) Romance has traces of Latin final /m/ only in a few monosyllabic words, such as French *rien* (nothing), from Latin *rem*, and Spanish *quien* (who), from Latin *quem*.

Word-final [s] and [t] also show signs of weakening. In the oldest inscriptions, the loss of the word-final letter *s* was quite common; yet spellings with the -*s* become the general rule later. Presumably this was because the *s* was indeed pronounced there, since most of Romance kept the Latin final [s]. Thus Spanish *hijos* < Latin *filios* (sons), *quieres* < *quaeris* (you seek), *dos* < *duos* (two), etc. It was the same in Old French, and indeed it still is in Modern French spelling, although in speech the language only preserves the sibilant in liaison, where it is voiced, such as the [z] that occurs at the end of the first word in the phrase *grands hommes*. Rumania and most of Italy lost the [-s], but this happened comparatively late, perhaps in the second half of the first millennium A.D.

The details of this process are still not clear. A quotation from Cicero (*Orator*, 161) is often adduced to show that at his time it was correct to pronounce word-final /s/, even in cases where older authors had felt it possible to omit it. If we take into consideration the usage of the Pompeii graffiti of A.D. 79, then we can deduce that final [s] was regularly present in their speech; and the later omission of the letter -*s* from inscriptions of a Vulgar Latin character is very much less frequent than is the omission of -m. It is only from the fifth and sixth centuries onward that the number of epigraphic examples of omission of -s grows appreciably, particularly in the Christian inscriptions from Rome and other parts of Italy; this period probably saw the origin of the future differentiation within Romania concerning the development of this feature.

An interesting theoretical debate has grown up on this issue. One of the most important of the twentieth-century Romance philologists, Walther von Wartburg, developed a hypothesis according to which the survival of the [-s] in the main Western Romance languages could be explained through sociocultural factors. His argument was that the Romanization of Gaul and Hispania happened on the basis of the speech of the cities and the more educated classes in society, who, in his view, pronounced the [-s] more than uneducated people and those in the countryside did. The reason for mentioning this idea is that it has been influential, although not everyone is convinced by it now; final [s] survived in places and at times where the level of education was not particularly high and the nature of the Romanization was in no sense particularly "urban," such as in Sardinia; and besides, as regards many other details, including the vowels, Hispania and Gaul followed, or even initiated, the general Vulgar Latin trends.

Word-final [t] seems to have been weaker than [-s]. Written forms lacking a -t are never very common, but they can be found from every period, particularly after a consonant. Thus *pos consulatum* for *post consulatum* (after the consulship), and *posuerun* for *posuerunt* (they put), are quite often found. There is a series of examples of loss of postvocalic [-t] in a famous graffito from Pompeii (CIL IV 1173, and its *Additamentum*, 204): *quisquis ama ualia, peria qui nosci amare*, which correctly written would have been *quisquis amat ualeat, pereat qui nescit amare* (long life to lovers, death to those who cannot love). Only a few traces of a final [t] remain in Romance now, and we can deduce that from the Late Latin period the final /t/ had been dropped from speech in some phonetic contexts, particularly before a word beginning with a consonant. Even so, it is still written in the oldest Romance texts from France; the *Strasbourg Oaths* (of 842) include the form *iurat* (swore), among others; there are forms such as *aimet* and *mandet* in the *Chanson de Roland*. Indeed, the letter -t persists in the official French orthography of a number of verb forms, and is still heard after verbs in liaison (such as *viennent-ils?* "are they coming?"). French is notably conservative in this respect; there is no trace now of [-t] or -*t* elsewhere.

When we consider the loss of final consonants, we have to bear in mind that even though their fate is indeed essentially a question of historical phonetics and phonology, it is also directly connected with phenomena on other levels of linguistic structure. These word-final sounds were also morphological elements, distinctive features of several parts of the Latin inflectional system. The presence of the final [s] (and of -*s* in writing) was enough in itself, for example, to distinguish inflections of nouns; examples of cases that only differed through the presence or absence of the [-s] included the dative and ablative singular form *domino* and the accusative plural form *dominos*; once the final [m] had gone, the [-s] served to distinguish the nominative singular form *dominus* from the accusative singular *dominum*; and in the conjugation of a large number of verbs, the [-s] was what distinguished the second-person singular indicative from the imperative, as with *laudas*, "you praise," and *lauda*, "praise!" It is probable that the phonetic and the morphological (and even the syntactic) evolution of the language interacted with each other in complex and detailed ways, the exact workings of which are still more or less unknown. It is possible that the need to keep necessary morphological distinctions affected or delayed the way in which consonants fell from word-final and other positions; but it is also possible that the weakening of the need for certain morphological and syntactic distinctions (such as between the accusative and the other cases, as we shall see in the next chapter) assisted the loss of word-final phonological distinctions between forms that had come in time to be functionally equivalent. This could be why these developments of the word-final consonants seem not to occur at a constant rate, and even at times to be reversed.

b) Palatalization

Some of the palatal consonants were particularly unstable in Vulgar Latin. We have already seen that this applies to the semiconsonantal

[j]; it also applied to the velar consonants [k] and [g], which involved occlusion of the air passage at the palate when the following vowel was a front vowel, [e] or [i]. This is natural; the palate (the roof of the mouth) has a relatively large surface area, so the tongue can be at or near many different parts of it, which means that the phonemes concerned can be realized phonetically across a whole range of variants and can easily be led to assimilate to the neighboring sounds. The converse is also true; several sounds whose point of articulation is near but not actually at the palate can easily be made to slip, because of the influence of a neighboring palatal sound, toward a palatal articulation; that is, in such cases the sounds palatalize.

The most widespread example of palatalization concerns the [k] before a [j] that had developed from unstressed [e] or [i] before another vowel (see above). Because of the neighboring [j], the point of articulation of the [k], originally velar, moved forward to become palatal, prepalatal, or even alveolar (that is, articulated on the ridge behind the top teeth), and hence to be pronounced in a less tense manner; thus the sound changed, perhaps via the intermediate sound [tj], to become the affricate [ts]. It is interesting to see that the pronunciation of [t] before a [j] relaxed in the same way, and over almost all the Romance area the resulting sound was also the same affricate [ts]. Our first sign of this development comes in the confusions between the letters *c* and *t* in such a context; for example, in Rome (*CIL* VI 34635) we find the written form *nacione* (nation), instead of *natione*, from before the advent of Christian epigraphy in the second half of the fourth century, and as time goes on these errors become ever more common. Grammarians of the fifth and sixth centuries are already mentioning the [ts] pronunciation and even present it as being normal. The letter *s* is also sometimes used to represent this affricate [ts], as, for example, in the written form *consiensia* (knowledge) instead of *conscientia* (*CIL* XII 2153). In spite of the parallel evolution and convergence of [kj] and [tj], there must have been a chronological difference between the two in at least some regions, for in large parts of the Romance world the results of the two developments are not entirely the same; here, when [tj] followed a vowel, it normally became a voiced affricate, as in Latin *puteum* (well) > Italian *pozzo*, or Latin *rationem* (reason) becoming French *raison* (in French, [ts] has since simplified and become a fricative), whereas [kj] following a vowel normally became a voiceless affricate, as when Vulgar Latin *facia* ("front," rather than the original *facies*) became Italian *faccia* and French *face* (also deaffricated since). In Hispania, however, there seems to have been no such difference in the evolution of the two; compare *puteum* > *pozo*, *faciem* > *haz*. This is a simplified picture, but even so it shows that the situation was complicated within late spoken Latin, and the details are still not all entirely clear.

On the other hand, inscriptions from the second century A.D. onward show more and more confusions in spelling between the following letters and digraphs, which seem at times to have appeared to be interchangeable: *i* when it represented [j], as in *maior*; *di* when it represented [dj] before a vowel; *g* when before [e], [i], or [j]; and even the letter *z*, which had been borrowed from the Greek alphabet. Examples of these confusions include the form *baptidiata* for *baptizata* (baptized) in a Christian inscription from Rome (*ICVR* [= *Inscriptiones Christianae Urbis Romae*] 927, of A.D. 459); the form *septuazinta* for *septuaginta* in Hispania (Vives 1969:52); *Ionisus* for *Dionysus* in Rome (*ICVR* 943, of the fourth or fifth century); *Genuarias* for *Ianuarias* ("January," *CIL* V 6209); *congiugi* for *coniugi* ("wife," *CIL* XI 1016, although perhaps the first *gi* here could be seen as a kind of anticipation of the second one). These confusions show us that the different sounds the separate symbols had once represented had undergone converging developments that led, by the end of the Empire, to the same sound, a prepalatal voiced affricate (roughly like the consonants in the English word *judge*). That sound is still there in Italian, where Latin *diurnum* (daily) > Italian *giorno* (day), *gentem* (people) > *gente*, *maiorem* (larger) > *maggiore*. In French this sound simplified later to a fricative alone in the words *jorn* (in Old French), *gent*, and *majeur*. But in this respect too, the evolution of Early Romance was neither straightforward nor uniform; in Spanish this originally common [dʒ] sound became even simpler, since the [j] is the variant that survived here in all cases before a stressed vowel: thus Latin *gemma* (bud) > *yema* (yolk), and *gelum* (ice) > *hielo*, which both begin with [j]; although before an initial unstressed vowel even that tended to disappear altogether, as in Latin *germanum* > Spanish *hermano* (brother), and Vulgar Latin *ienuarium* (rather than the original *ianuarium*, "January") > Spanish *enero*.

In most of the Romance Languages [k] became a sibilant sound before syllabic [e] and [i] (that is, when not shortened to [j]), but a different sibilant in different areas. Thus Latin *cera*, pronounced [kéra], became Italian *cera*, now pronounced [tʃéra] ([ʃ] represents the palatal sibilant fricative, the sound spelled *sh* in English), French *cire*, now pronounced [síːr], and Spanish *cera*, now pronounced [θéra], from Old Spanish [tséra]. Comparing the Romance developments leads us to believe, despite a shortage of clear textual or epigraphic evidence, that this assibilation process had also begun before the end of the Empire.

c) Intervocalic Consonants

The weakening of intervocalic consonants is mentioned here because it is an important development that cannot be ignored, but it needs to be made clear from the start that this was not a pan-Romance phenomenon. Apart from the fricativization of intervocalic [b], which happened over a large area, this weakening only happened in part of the Empire, and, on the whole, in the postimperial period.

This word "weakening" is a convenient metaphor because it describes the development accurately. It was in essence a process of assimilation of the consonant to the neighboring vowels. Unvoiced consonants between vowels became voiced; voiced intervocalic consonants became fricative; and eventually some intervocalic consonants, in some areas, disappeared from speech altogether. The weakening of [-b-] is the only general case, and thus the only one that we can deduce began at an early period; after its plosive realization relaxed and the lips were no longer completely closed at the start of its articulation, the pronunciation of the original voiced bilabial plosive /b/ became the fricative [β] and thus easy to confuse with the [β] that had developed from the semiconsonantal /w/ once it lost its velar component (as described above). Written forms such as *siui* for *sibi* (for himself), or the other way round, such as *uiba* for *uiua* (living), are common all over the area from the first century A.D.

It is possible, in fact, that this phenomenon is a part of a wider development, a "crisis" that affected all the labials, not only in intervocalic position. In wide areas of the Empire—in Italy, the Balkans, North Africa; much less so in Hispania, and hardly at all in Gaul—spelling confusion between *b* and *u* (usually writing *b* instead of *u*, rather than the other way round) was common in word-initial position and after a consonant as well. Later inscriptions offer many examples of the form *bixit* (lived) for *uixit*, and *serbus* (slave) for *seruus*; these spellings are a consequence of the pronunciation of the /w/ as [β] mentioned above. This is a complicated process, which can be traced in Romance; regarding [rw], for example, there are forms like the Italian *serbare* (keep) from Latin *seruare*, and French *corbeau* (crow) from a Vulgar Latin diminutive of *coruus* (which also led to Rumanian *corb*); and in initial position there is the neat example of Rumanian *bătrîn* (old) from Latin *ueteranus*. In Gascony and several areas of southern Italy [b] and semiconsonantal [w] evolved convergently into the same sound in word-initial position. Modern Spanish has also evolved regularly this way, but in this case it seems less likely that the process began during the Vulgar Latin period, considering that the spelling confusion between the letters *b* and *u* is relatively rare in Hispania. In intervocalic position, however, there is much more unanimity, since here the original plosive [b] has now become a fricative nearly everywhere; for example, Vulgar Latin *caballum* (horse) is now French *cheval* and Italian *cavallo*, with the labiodental fricative [v], and Spanish *caballo*, with the bilabial fricative [β].

As regards the other unvoiced intervocalic plosive consonants, it is famously the case that in the eastern areas, in Rumania and central and southern Italy, these consonants are still usually unvoiced, whereas they have weakened to various degrees further west. Thus Latin *mutare* (to change) became *muta* in Rumanian and *mutare* in Italian; although there is another Italian word *mudare*, also from Latin *mutare*, used of snakes changing their skin, this is usually thought to have been borrowed into Italian from a Northern dialect, since in northern Italy and further west the [t] regularly voiced to [d], as is still the case in Spanish *mudar*; later, in France, the [d] disappeared, leading to Modern French *muer*. Scholars have tried to find the first stages of these developments, in other consonants as well as the [-t-], reflected in the epigraphy of the Empire; but the few cases that seem to document this development need to be treated with care, in fact. The earliest definite examples are from the sixth century: for example, *sub ista labidem marmorea* for *sub istam lapidem marmoream* ("beneath this marble stone," CIL XIII 5252), which attests not only a [b] rather than the original [p] in the noun *labidem* but also its use as a feminine rather than the original masculine (although this was found in archaic times also). There are just a few isolated and unclear examples of *-d-* for *-t-* from the time of the Empire that may attest the change from [-t-] to [-d-], but these are only frequent and clear from the seventh century onward. Merovingian documents offer examples such as the form *podibat* for *potebat* ("could," the Vulgar Latin replacement for original *poterat*: see section 5.2 below), and *rodatico* for *rotatico* (wheel tax). So it seems that the weakening of the intervocalic consonants started for the most part when the different Romance-speaking areas were already separate from each other politically.

d) Consonant Clusters

In general, Vulgar Latin simplified consonant clusters. Not every possible combination of consonants need be exemplified here. One of the most common was the reduction, in spelling, of the cluster *ns* to a simple *s*, reflecting the fact that the /n/ was no longer consonantal, or even that it was absent. The inscriptions have countless examples of this: *mensis* written as *mesis* (month), *sponsus* written as *sposus* (husband), *consul* written as *cosul*. Similarly, the clusters [mn], [kt] (spelled *ct*), and [ks] (spelled *x*) assimilated the first consonant into the pronunciation of the second in the cluster; at first, probably, this led to long [n:], [t:], and [s:], but these soon slimmed down into [n], [t], and [s]. These developments are then reflected in spellings such as *onibus* for *omnibus* (dative-ablative plural of *omnes*, "all," CIL X 477), *inditione* for *indictione* ("indiction," CIL V 5429), and *bissit* for *uixit* ("lived," from Rome, ICVR 5030). Similarly, groups of three consonants slimmed down to two, usually losing the consonant in the middle; thus we see *imtores* for *emptores* ("buyers," from Rome, ICVR 4279). These changes can be seen subsequently in the development of these words in Romance; Latin *mensem*, for example, became Portuguese *mês*, Spanish and Catalan *mes*, Old French *meis* (> Modern *mois*), and Italian *mese*. The development of [kt], and to a lesser extent [ks], was complex, different in different areas. In the East the [k] assimilated to the [t], leading in Italy to [tt], where Latin *octo* (eight) became *otto*, and *noctem* (night) > *notte*, and in Rumania to the group [pt], as in *opt* (eight) and *noapte* (night). In the West, the [k] in the cluster palatalized to [j], and in French this led to the diphthongization of the previous vowel, such that these words are now *huit* and *nuit*. The Spanish words developed further to *ocho* and *noche*, with a new affricate, [tʃ]. There is Latin textual evidence of the [tt], as in *lattucae*, "lettuces," for *lactucae* (CIL III 807, of the year 301), but not of the palatalization, which suggests that that development started later.

Many groups consisting of a consonant and the semivowel [j] simplified also. Several of these groups seem never to have been stable anyway, which is why we find spellings such as *facunt* for *faciunt* ("they make," CIL III 3551). A curse tablet from Pannonia regularly uses the form *aduersaro* for *aduersario* (enemy), and there are many other such spellings. These developments are continued in Romance, such that Latin *parietem* (wall) turns up as *parede* in Portugal, *pared* in Spain, *paroi* in France, and *parete* in Italy. The semiconsonantal [w] weakened after a [k], which led to increasing spelling confusions between the letters *qu* (originally representing [kw]) and *c* (originally representing [k]), as in *quesquentis* for *quiescentis* ("of the person who rests here," from Rome in the year 435, ICVR 529); and the single letter *q*, without *u* (which had never been correct), is also often found, both for *c*, as in *qurpus* for *corpus* ("body," CIL V 6244), and for *qu*, as in *qarta* for *quarta* (a personal name, CIL III 5479). In Romance, [kw] lost the [w] in most words, as in Italian *chi* and French *qui* ([ki], "who") from Latin *qui* ([kwi], and Spanish *quien* ([kjen], "who") from Latin *quien*, although in some places it often survived before an [a], as in Spanish *cual* ([kwal]) and Italian *quale* ([kwale], "which") from Latin *qualem*.

A final group of examples of intervocalic consonant weakening concerns geminates such as [ss], [tt], and [nn], which often simplify to a single consonant. Toward the end of the Empire in particular, we find written forms such as *posim* for *possim* ("I can," subjunctive), *puela* for *puella* (girl), and *anorum* for *annorum* (of the years); these examples are taken from Christian inscriptions in northern Italy, but similar cases can be found in all regions. This too coincides with the evidence from Romance, which tends to simplify these clusters nearly everywhere, although the spelling sometimes hides this fact, preserving the double letters for what has become a single sound, as, for example, in French *mettre* ("to put," from Latin *mittere*), which represents a spoken [mɛtr] with a single [t].

5

INFLECTIONAL MORPHOLOGY

1. Nominal Morphology

Latin possessed a rich system of nominal morphology, which at first sight seems well balanced. There were three genders of nouns, masculine, feminine, and neuter. There were five main declensional classes, traditionally numbered from one to five: the first included nouns with the nominative singular ending in *-a* and the genitive ending in *-ae*, such as *terra, terrae*, "land"; the second, such as *dominus, domini*, "Lord," and *bellum, belli*, "war"; the third, such as *miles, militis*, "soldier," and *nauis, nauis*, "ship"; the fourth, such as *senatus, senatus*, "senate," and *cornu, cornus*, "horn"; and the fifth, such as *res, rei*, "thing." Adjectives either followed the inflections of the first two declensions (e.g., *durus*, "hard," masculine, *dura* feminine, and *durum* neuter) or those of the third (e.g., *grandis*, "great," masculine and feminine, and *grande*, neuter), although a few special rules governed the declension of adjectives of the second type. The declension of the pronouns coincided only partly with that of the nominals, and will be treated separately below.

Each declension had five inflectional cases in the singular and five in the plural; these are traditionally known as the nominative (for the subject of the sentence), the accusative (for the direct object), the genitive (possessive), the dative (for the indirect object), and the ablative. Certain categories of nouns also had a vocative or a locative inflection. But this system was not as economically organized as it might seem, because, like the inflectional systems of most such languages, some of the endings had asymmetrical distribution; for example, in the first declension the genitive and dative singular inflections were the same (as in *terrae*); in the second declension the dative and ablative singular inflections were the same (as in *domino*); and the nominative and accusative singular inflections coincided in the second and fourth declensions, but none of the others did (*dominus* and *senatus*, *dominum* and *senatum*). Nor was there any particular correlation between an inflection and its function; for example, the -*i* inflection of the second declension marked both the genitive singular and the nominative plural, while in the third declension the same inflection marked the dative singular and, in nouns with the theme vowel in -*i*-, the ablative singular also. Conversely, the same function could be fulfilled by several totally different inflections; for example, the genitive singular was expressed by four (or five, depending on how we define them) separate inflections in the five declensions: that is, the forms *terrae*, *domini*, *militis*, *senatus*, and *rei* are all genitive singular.

This lack of strict symmetry or exact parallelism in the system was, paradoxically, helpful; phrases such as *boni milites*, "good soldiers," could only be masculine plural, even though each of the words was inflectionally ambiguous in itself; *bonos milites* could only be accusative plural; and *boni militis* could only be genitive singular. Even so, the possibility for confusion was large, and it cannot have been an easy system to master perfectly. For example, from the earliest written texts we find uncertainty whether the ablative of such third-declension nouns as *nauis* should be *naui* or *naue*; and the genitive singular form of the fourth-declension nouns such as *senatus* could often appear with -*i* rather than the correct -*us*, representing a long [uː] (this is clearly due to a process of analogy, the tendency to create one common form within two paradigms that already coincide in part); Classical literary texts, however, usually present the "correct" form.

In order to understand what was to happen to the declension system in Vulgar Latin, we need to appreciate these aspects of the original system;

for in texts of a "Vulgar" character we can see clear signs that this system is breaking down. Some of the categories seem to be disappearing, and the inflectional morphemes that are still being used are at times inappropriate. After the end of the Empire, this process accelerates, and most of the earliest direct written representations of the Romance languages show that the whole system has by then simplified almost as far as it could; each noun has one singular form and one plural form only, with only a few irregularities in the vowels or in the formation of the plural remaining as distant echoes of the Latin declensions. The well-known exception to this is Gallo-Romance (and perhaps medieval Rhaeto-Romance, about which we know very little), since for several centuries Old French and Old Occitan were going to keep a two-case system, in both the singular and the plural, consisting of one form used for the verbal subject (descending from the original nominative) and another for all other cases (usually descending from the original accusative). This Gallo-Romance system did not involve every noun, since most feminine nouns (such as French *terre*, "land," from Latin *terra*) had already slimmed down to one form for the singular and another for the plural by the time of the earliest written texts in Romance form; and so had most of the masculine nouns that had once been neuter, such as Old French *cors*, from Latin *corpus*, "body." Rumanian is a different kind of exception to the general development, since there feminine nouns preserved a distinction between a nominative-accusative and a genitive-dative inflection.

The loss of inflections was less radical and rather different in the pronouns; but otherwise, the way in which nominal inflections developed in Vulgar Latin was to lead to systems in Romance that were quite unlike the Latin ones; this was a fundamental change in the system of the grammar and deserves to be examined in detail.

The most important change, of course, that which was going to have the widest and most complex repercussions on the system inherited from the original Latin, was the loss of a genuine inflectional system. Before we consider how and why this happened, it is worth remembering that this process of reduction did not in fact begin with Vulgar Latin, since Classical Latin itself represented a simplification of the system it had inherited. Classical Latin had fewer inflectional categories than Indo-European had had; it also lost one of its categories of number, for Indo-European had had a dual number, as well as singular and plural, for explicitly referring to two entities. Not only that, but certain inflections that had been distinct in Archaic Latin had come to be pronounced the same way, as a result of phonetic change; for example, the Classical second-declension dative and ablative singular inflection in -o had once been two distinct endings: -oi, dative, and -od, ablative; similarly, the -i of the genitive singular and nominative plural nouns of this same declension had descended from two different inflections. Vulgar Latin continued this process and led it eventually to its logical conclusion, but this was an ancient process in itself that did not originate with Vulgar Latin.

The phonetic developments that overtook spoken Latin in post-Classical times were enough in themselves to weaken the distinctive boundaries between a number of inflections. When the final [-m] had gone and the distinction between long and short [a] was no longer made, the nominative singular *rosa* (rose), the accusative singular *rosam* (both with originally short [a]), and the ablative singular *rosa* (with originally long [a:]) all represented the same pronunciation; when short [u] and long [o:] ceased to be distinguished, then the pronunciation of accusative singular *dominum* and dative and ablative singular *domino* came to be the same; and there are many other cases in the other declensions, such as *militem* (accusative singular) and *milite* (ablative singular). The language must have reached this stage by the fifth century at the latest, and by then the first-declension singular already had only two distinct spoken forms, [rósa] (written *rosa* or *rosam*) and [róse] (written *rosae*); the masculine nouns of the second declension had only three singular inflectional forms, [-os], [-o], and [-i]; the third-declension nouns no longer had a distinction between accusative and ablative singular, and different forms had other coincidences depending on their stem.

It would not be right, though, to conclude, as many of the Romance scholars of the nineteenth century tended to conclude, that the loss of the case system was entirely caused by phonetic developments. Several inflections would have been fully capable of preserving their phonetic individuality, despite all the developments. The distinction between the nominative *dominus* or *res* and the other inflectional forms depended on the survival of the final [-s], but genitives such as *militis* had also ended in [-s], yet they disappeared nonetheless. Similarly, the originally long [iː] remained a distinctive vowel throughout the Empire, and afterward continued to be so almost everywhere, so there was no phonetic reason for the second-declension genitive singular inflection and the third-declension dative singular inflection, both originally [-iː], to be confused with any others. Indeed, the cases we have seen so far are overwhelmingly in the singular; in the plural, the great majority of the phonetic distinctions on which the inflectional distinctions depended were stable and survived; for example, plural forms such as the nominative-accusative *patres* (fathers), the genitive *patrum*, and the dative-ablative *patribus* could have remained in existence and phonetically separate to this day, in any part of the Romance world. The distinctions that survived the phonetic developments were about as many in number as those that had eroded, and if the tendency to weaken these distinctions was the one that prevailed, then this must have been due to other reasons in addition to the phonetic ones. We can only deduce, then, that functional factors were the ones that led to the eventual definitive abandonment of all the old inflectional systems even where the inflections were still distinctive.

Indeed, we can notice in Late Latin texts an increasing number of confusions between inflections that were formally quite distinct. It was common, for example, to be confused between the accusative or the ablative; in such circumstances, the accusative was more often used inappropriately, instead of an originally correct ablative, than vice versa. The accusative seems to have been felt to be a kind of "prepositional case," and as a result it often appears in Vulgar texts after prepositions that normally required the noun to be in the ablative: examples of the prepositions involved include *cum*, "with," as in *cum filios suos tres* (CIL VIII 3933, "with his three children"); *a* and *ab*, as in *posita a fratres* (CIL VIII 20300, "put up by his brothers"); and *pro*, as in *pro se et suos* (CIL XII 1185, "for himself and his family"); these examples are chosen from the hundreds that exist. There are also, of course, occasions on which the ablative case appears instead of a correct accusative, particularly after *ob* (because of), probably due to the influence of *pro* (for the purpose of); the phrase *ob meritis*, "because of his merits," instead of *ob merita*, is commonly found in the inscriptions. Some prepositions admitted use with both cases anyway, originally involving a difference in meaning, such as *sub* (under) and *in* (in), where the ablative answers the question *ubi?* (where?), to indicate the place where something is to be found, and the accusative answers the question *quo?* (where to?), indicating the direction of a movement. This semantic distinction is not always clear in real life and is often absent from the Vulgar Latin evidence: the phrases *sub hoc titulo* (the originally correct use) and *sub hunc titulum*, meaning "beneath this tombstone," seem in effect to be free alternatives in Christian epigraphy; and there are converse cases such as *iuit in caelis*, used for the originally correct *iuit in caelos*, "he went to heaven."

These examples demonstrate just one part of the great extension that took place in the use of the accusative. The accusative was originally used for the direct object of a transitive verb, and transitivity itself increased. Many verbs in Classical Latin were followed by a noun in the genitive, dative, or ablative case, but in Vulgar texts these verbs tend to take an accusative. For example, the verb *maledicere* (to curse) took a dative noun in the Classical language, but it is used transitively with an accusative in Petronius. The accusative comes to substitute for the ablative after a large number of verbs, and in Christian authors there are phrases such as *caruerunt hanc . . . deterrimam labem*, "they were free of this very serious dishonor," where *carere*, "lack," is followed by the noun phrase in the accusative rather than the ablative, *hac deterrima labe* (this phrase is from the *De laude martyrii*, 6, wrongly attributed to Cyprian); similarly, the fourth-century writer Lucifer of Cagliari wrote *frui felicitatem perpetuam* (enjoy everlasting happiness), with the accusative, rather than *felicitate perpetua*, with the ablative, in his *De Athanasio* (I.20). The increasing occurrence of the accusative as the general case for all nonsubject uses becomes clear, toward the end of the Empire, in the appearance of a completely new construction, the accusative absolute, modeled on the traditional ablative absolute and nearly always carrying out the same function, that of representing a temporally subordinate clause; a good example of this comes from the sixth-century writer Gregory of Tours, who wrote (*Vitae Patrum*, VII.4), *quod opus perfectum . . . conuocat presbiteros* ("once this work was completed"—in the accusative—"he calls together the priests").

But we should note that despite this increasing confusion in the use of the inflectional cases, the accusative and nominative are in most places rarely confused in the inscriptions. In Gaul, they are hardly ever confused even in the Merovingian texts (of the sixth and seventh centuries). Recent research suggests, however, that the distinction between nominative and accusative was beginning, particularly in Africa, to become unclear by the end of the Empire, and then a bit later in parts of Italy and Hispania. The evidence for this usually takes the form of ostensibly inappropriate uses of the accusative, rather than vice versa. Thus we find a Christian inscription reading *Crescensa . . . cui filios et nepotes obitum fecerunt* (CIL VIII 21540), "for whom his sons and grandsons celebrated the funeral rites," where the accusative *filios* is used instead of the nominative *filii*, and another reading *fecit frater eor[um] maiorem* (CIL VIII 20536), "their elder brother made this," where *maiorem* is used instead of *maior*. Similar examples can be found in later texts from Italy, particularly in legal documents from the eighth century on, and in some late Vulgar texts from Visigothic Spain.

We also find, however, a group of examples that show a more regular substitution of an accusative for a nominative as the subject of the verb; the plural inflection of first-declension feminine nouns ending in *-a*, used as the subject of the verb, is often written with *-as* rather than the original *-ae*. Examples of this form have surfaced in most of the provinces of the Empire, dating from the first century A.D. onward. A curse tablet from Africa (Audollent 222, already quoted above) contains the imprecation *inimicorum meorum linguas aduersus me ommutescant*, "may the tongues of my enemies who speak against me be silent," where the form *linguas* appears instead of *linguae*; in an epitaph from Pannonia we find a whole collection of examples (CIL III 3551, perhaps of the third century): *hic quescunt* [for *quiescunt*] *duas matres duas filias. . . et aduenas II paruolas*, "here lie two mothers, two daughters . . . and two young foreign girls." This usage only arrives in Gaul after the fifth century, but then it spreads quickly; the situation in Gaul shows clearly that this use of nominatives ending in *-as* is only the result of formal morphological confusion, rather than a more general confusion between nominatives and accusatives, since no similar confusions are attested between the relevant inflections of nouns of other types; there is hardly a written example of confusion between singular *dominus* and *dominum*, or plural *domini* and *dominos*, etc.

The origins of this use of *-as* for subject nouns have been much debated. There is good reason to think of it as having begun as a dialect feature: Oscan and Umbrian, the two important Italic languages related to Latin, had a first-declension nominative plural ending *-as*, such that, for example, Oscan *scriftas* corresponds to Latin *scriptae*, and the archaic Latin texts contain several nominatives like this. These dialectal uses, isolated to begin with, could have been helped to spread by the analogy of those declensions in which the nominative and accusative were already identical in the plural, such as *milites* and *res*.

At the same time as the spread of the semantic and functional confusion between the accusative inflections and, in particular, those of the ablative, the roles of the genitive and dative cases also became less clearly distinct from each other. In fact, the dative had all along been available to express possessive relationships, both in such constructions as *mihi est* ("I have [something]": literally, "it's to me") and in the adnominal use known as the ethic dative, or the dative of interest, which could often be used to refer to a relationship that could just as well have been referred to with a genitive—for example, in Virgil's *Aeneid*, X, 134–35: *qualis gemma micat fuluum quae diuidit aurum, / aut collo decus aut capiti* (it shines like a gem set in yellow gold, an ornament either for the neck or for the head). Here, *collo* and *capiti* are datives, but could as well have been genitives, since from the semantic point of view they are effectively possessives ("of the neck or of the head"). In Late Latin texts, this possessive use of nouns in the dative case became increasingly common, not only in technical and other Vulgar works, but even in works with some pretensions to literary elegance. In the *Mulomedicina Chironis*, for example, we read *cui caput erigere si uolueris* (316, "if you wanted to lift the animal's head," literally, "lift the head to the animal"), but we can also find the construction in works such as the poems of Commodian: for example, *nascanturque quasi denuo suae matri de uentre* (*Instructiones*, II.10.7, "that they should be reborn, so to speak, from the belly of the mother," where the mother appears in the dative as *matri*). Eventually, the dative came to replace the genitive in nonpossessive functions as well, as can be seen in the phrase used by Gregory of Tours, *cui . . . supra meminimus* ("which we mentioned above," *Historia Francorum*, II.9); here *cui* is dative, but originally the verb *memini* required a genitive case in the object noun. Some sporadic confusions also occur in the other direction, when a genitive case is used where we would expect the dative, but the general drift of the process is clear enough; gradually, the dative was taking over from the genitive.

I could quote many other examples of confusions between nominal inflections, but I have already cited more than enough to show that these are genuine morphological confusions, caused by the progressive loss of the semantic distinctions between the inflections in question, that there was in the relevant instances a kind of increasing functional equivalence between the oblique (nonnominative) cases. This helps us to understand why the inflectional system was going to disappear completely; the weakening of the phonological distinctions between several forms was aided and abetted and eventually pushed to the limit by the weakening of the semantic frontiers between their functions. The genitive and dative inflections, which were formally distinct in most nouns, came to be widely interchangeable because of the increasing equivalence in their functions in speech. The dative and the ablative had clearly separated functions but, in most nouns, identical inflections, particularly in the plurals ending in *-is* or *-bus*, but also in the second-declension singular forms ending in *-o* and many nouns and almost all adjectives of the third-declension singular ending in *-i*; in this way the uncertainty between genitive and dative usage could spread to the ablative as well. Then the incursions made by the accusative into the areas hitherto colonized by the other inflections, most notably the ablative, ended up by leading to general uncertainty concerning the proper use of all four of them. The lack of symmetry, the lack of exact parallels in the system, which we observed at the start and which survived in spite of the subsequent phonetic changes, helped to spread the different kinds of confusion from one declension to another and between the singular and the plural; and where clear formal distinctions survived in one declension, as between the dative and ablative singular of nouns of the first declension (*-ae* and *-a*), these too came to be weakened semantically as a result of the influence of the other declensions in which any distinction had either never existed or no longer existed.

To sum up, it is reasonable to deduce that halfway through the first millennium a.d. the use of the old declension systems was much reduced in speech. The details of the process, insofar as we can glimpse them now, could well have varied from region to region. In Gaul, and probably in at least the western part of the Alps as well, there was only one oblique case in speech (that is, other than the nominative), usually descended phonetically from the original accusative and represented in writing by one or other of the inherited inflections; in the most Vulgar texts, it looks as if the form chosen was selected from these more or less at random, whereas comparatively educated writers tended to choose the inflection that had been required in Classical Latin.

When we read, in the oldest version of the Salic Law (the Franks' lawbook, written in Latin, which was edited in a number of written versions from the first half of the sixth century on), the phrase *qui cum rege ancilla mechatus fuerit* (*Pactus Legis Salicae*, XXV.4[2]: "anyone who had sex with the king's slavegirl"), we are confronted with the form *rege*: from the strictly morphological point of view, this could be interpreted as an ablative, indeed traditionally written as *rege*, or as an accusative that has lost its [m], traditionally *regem*, but in this case the form is fulfilling a genitive function, "of the king," or perhaps an ethic dative function, "to the king." It is, in reality, the written representation, one of four available in the inherited repertoire of written inflexions, of what was by then a single oblique case. This stage, containing only a nominative and an oblique inflection in the singular and the plural, still survives in the two-case declensions of Old French and Old Occitan texts (and probably in the contemporary but unwritten Western Rhaeto-Romance as well). On the other hand, as mentioned above, in some areas, in Africa and probably parts of Italy and Hispania, the nominative and the accusative came together earlier than in Gaul, so it is probable that the Romance spoken in these areas, at least in some declensions, ended up quite soon with just one inflection for each noun in the singular and another in the plural, which effectively means that in those regions there was no longer a system of inflections at all.

The picture just given of the main western and central areas of the Romance-speaking world implies a certain simplification of complex events, but it seems to be essentially accurate. The speech of more educated groups, influenced by daily contact with biblical and liturgical texts that still maintained the ancient inflections, may have been a bit different; to them the phonetically stable and distinctive endings such as *-ibus* (dative and ablative plural of third-declension nouns) and *-arum* and *-orum* (genitive plural of first- and second-declension nouns respectively) probably sounded solemn and important, even if also archaic. It has been noted that even in the most markedly "vulgar" Merovingian texts, these forms, when they are found (and they are), are used in the normal way, with their correct functions. This may well have also applied to Italy and Hispania, as well as to Gaul.

It looks as if the developments were slightly different in the East. Late inscriptions from the Balkans contain far more possessive datives than elsewhere, which probably attests to the survival in these regions of a dative-genitive inflection opposed to all the other cases. This development could be what explains the presence in Modern Rumanian of a two-case system in feminine nouns, in which ţare (< terrae, dative and genitive) is opposed to ţară (< both terra, nominative, and terram, accusative).

Summarizing what we have established so far about the history of the Latin declension system in speech, we are able to conclude that its disappearance can reasonably be attributed to a combination of several factors. The continual developments that overtook the phonetic system helped to weaken or even abolish the distinctions in speech between several inflections; the functional frontiers between several cases had been unclear all along, and these also weakened further, to the extent that several inflections came to be interchangeable even when the phonetic distinctions between them were not in danger of being eroded; and in addition, analogical changes arose in an attempt to remedy the lack of symmetry between the different declension types, helping to spread confusions from one declension to another. But despite all this, we can presume that these destructive forces could not have been successful if the nominal inflectional system had been an essential part of the language's means of expression, if it had in real life been a grammatical device without which speech was going to be full of ambiguities and misunderstandings. We shall see in the next section that the verb system also was the victim of the same phonetic developments and similar functional uncertainties (which can operate in any part of the language) but that it survived throughout this period nonetheless, in a state very similar to its original one. So if the nominal inflectional system disappeared, this can only imply that its preservation was unnecessary; the language as a whole had other expressive devices already available, and those could be used instead to fulfil satisfactorily the functions once expressed by the inflections.

The most important of these alternative expressive mechanisms involved the use of prepositions. Even in Classical times, some inflections and prepositional phrases were either entirely or partly equivalent; for "to send a letter to someone" they could either use the dative, as in *mittere litteras alicui*, or the preposition *ad* and the accusative, as in *mittere litteras ad aliquem*. Constructions such as *e patre egregio natus*, "born of an eminent father," and *summo loco natus*, "born in a high place," were equally acceptable, and meant the same in practice, whether the *e* was there or not; similarly, *e Britannia profectus* and *Roma profectus*, "having set out from Britain / from Rome," were semantically identical. Prepositional phrases had in any event some important advantages over the use of inflections without prepositions, which must have meant that they were the usual automatic choices in speech, particularly in the speech of newly Romanized groups with no tradition yet of literary education, who were probably clumsier in the manipulation of the complex machinery of preposition-free inflections. The phrases were morphologically more straightforward, since the prepositions only had a single invariant form. They came to be used more and more with the accusative case, which was easy to use and created no ambiguity (since the preposition carried the meaning). On the other hand, both the forms and the distribution of the inflections were disconcertingly complicated. From the functional point of view, in fact, the prepositions, each with a more homogeneous meaning than an inflection had (since there were more of them), were clearer and more precise than the naked inflection, even though the phrase was usually longer and, perhaps, lacking in nuances. It is not at all surprising, then, that statistically the average number of prepositional phrases per length of text doubles from Archaic to Late Latin. The increase in prepositional usage would have been even more marked in speech.

Prepositional phrases with *de* were what usually replaced the genitive inflections; both the partitive use of the genitive, as in Benedict of Nursia's *Regula monachorum* (of about A.D. 540), 39: *de eadem libra tertia pars . . . seruetur* (that a third of the same weight of bread . . . should be kept in reserve), and the possessive use, as in Theodosius's *De situ terrae sanctae*, also of the sixth century, 11: *monasterium . . . de castas* (a convent of nuns), where we can also note that the *de* is followed by the accusative inflection, in *castas*, rather than by the originally correct ablative.

The alternative to using the dative case was usually a prepositional phrase comprising *ad* and the accusative. This had been true from the earliest texts: for example, Plautus's *Captiui*, 360: *quae ad patrem uis nuntiari* (what you want to be announced to your father), contains *nuntiare ad* and the accusative *patrem*, but is followed shortly after in line 400 by the alternative, *nuntiare* and the dative *patri*, in the same context: *numquid aliud uis patri nuntiari?* (do you want something else to be announced to your father?); but it is only in the Late Latin period that the prepositional phrases begin to be common. The sentence *locutus est ad illos* is a normal way of expressing "he spoke to them" in the oldest of the Bible translations, for example; from the *Mulomedicina Chironis* we can quote, inter alia, *ad eos des manducare* (454, "give them something to eat"), and phrases of this kind become increasingly common after the end of the Empire.

The replacement of the ablative by prepositional phrases was understandably a more complicated process than the replacement of the dative and genitive, since the functions of the ablative had all along been more complex than the others; with temporal meaning, the ablative often gave way to phrases with *in*, such as *in hoc tempore* for *hoc tempore*, "at this time"; ablatives of manner were replaced by phrases using *cum*, "with"; ablatives of cause by prepositional phrases using *per* or *propter*, "because of"; and similarly in other uses.

To sum this section up, all the functions that had been fulfilled by the inflections, other than the subject function expressed by the nominative and the direct-object function expressed by the accusative, came more and more to be generally expressed by prepositional phrases instead, which replaced the comparatively slippery and disorganized case system. (Later, in Ibero-Romance and Rumanian, the direct-object function would often be marked by a preposition also.) This shows that the loss of the declension system was not an isolated event in itself; it was just one aspect, the negative aspect, so to speak, of a much wider process of transformation that affected the whole grammatical organization of sentences.

Before we leave the nouns and turn to the adjectives, we should add that the loss of the inflections had an important consequence for the number of declension patterns. The fifth and fourth declensions had never contained a large number of nouns, and now, with the reduction of the inflections, they were no longer very distinctive. Nouns of the fourth declension, such as *senatus*, *fructus*, "fruit," and a few ending in *-u*, originally with genitive *-us* ([-u:s]), were taken into the second one, on the pattern of *dominus*; these two declensions had had the same inflections anyway in the nominative and accusative singular. Similarly, feminine nouns of the fifth declension, such as *facies* (face) and *rabies* (fury), with a long [-e:], which had had genitives ending in *-ei*, moved to the declension most closely associated with the feminine gender, the first, with nominative singular endings in *-a*. The Romance languages have preserved a few vestigial traces of the original declension in *-es*: for example, French *rien*, "nothing," comes from the accusative form of *res*, *rem*, and Spanish *haz* and Old Occitan *fatz* derive from *faciem*; but French *face* and Italian *faccia* come from the later Latin form *facia*, and that is the commoner pattern. This reduction may well have started much earlier, in fact, since right from the start Latin texts show that a certain number of nouns were vacillating between the second and fourth declensions, or between the first and fifth. Even so, despite these occasional uncertainties, the distinction between the three surviving types of nouns remained firm; that is, first-declension nouns such as *rosa*, second-declension nouns such as *dominus*, and third-declension nouns such as *miles* remained distinct.

The inflections developed the same way in adjectives as in nouns. Latin adjectives were either formed with the endings of the first declension, for the feminine, and the second declension, for the masculine and the neuter (e.g., masculine *bonus*, feminine *bona*, and neuter *bonum*, "good"), or with the endings of the third-declension nouns with nominative *-is*, where the masculine and feminine were identical but the neuter was distinct in the nominative and accusative; thus *uiridis*, "green," had a neuter form *uiride*, an ablative singular for all genders in *uiridi*, a neuter nominative and accusative form *uiridia*, and a genitive plural for all genders in *uiridium*. On the whole, these two types kept themselves separate all through the Late Latin period, with a few uncertainties here and there (such as the form *acrum* for the neuter of the third declension attested by the *Appendix Probi*, 41: *acre non acrum*). Thus Italian still has masculine *buono* formally separate from feminine *buona* but (in standard Italian, at least) *grande* and *verde* for both genders; similarly, Spanish *bueno*, *buena*, *grande*, and *verde*. Where this pattern broke down, as in French, in which we now have masculine *grand* and *vert* but a separate feminine form, *grande* and *verte*, it happened later, after the separation into separate Romance languages. (The French feminines *grande* and *verte* are analogical forms, following the model of the more frequent *bon*, Old French *bone*, type; the stem consonant had been adapted to that of the masculines, which is now only orthographic.) It is worth highlighting this relative stability in the distinct types of adjective declension, since it shows that the overall patterns of simplification in the system of nominal morphology (that is, adjectives and nouns together) were somewhat selective; the desire for simplification was not felt equally strongly in all parts of the system. In the inflections themselves, the simplification was radical, coherent, and complete, but it was less far-reaching in the reduction of the types of noun declension and of genders (as we shall see below). This suggests that the processes were an integral part of the development of the whole morpho-syntactic system of the language and cannot be understood in isolation from the wider trends.

The development of the grades of comparison in adjectives is interesting (and similar in its pattern to several other developments). In Latin, the comparative form of an adjective was usually created by the addition to the adjectival stem of the suffix *-ior* (neuter form *-ius*), comparable to the English *-er*: thus *facilis, facilior* (easy, easier), *rapidus, rapidior* (quick, quicker), *pulcher, pulchrior* (beautiful, more beautiful). Similarly, the superlative form was often created by adding the suffix *-issimus*, comparable to the English *-est*, to the stem, as in *rapidissimus* (quickest), although adjectival stems ending in [l] or [r] had different forms, as did *facillimus* (easiest) and *pulcherrimus* (most beautiful). Some common adjectives and their derived adverbs acquired different stems in these formations: for example, *bonus* (good), *melior* (better), *optimus* (best); *magnus* (big), *maior* (bigger), *maximus* (biggest). But alongside these mechanisms, there had always existed the alternative of marking the comparative with the adverb *magis*, or less commonly *plus*, meaning "more," accompanying the normal positive form of the adjective; *maxime* (most) was similarly available as an alternative for the superlative. Examples include, from the Vulgate, *Sapientia* (8.20): *et cum essem magis bonus ueni ad corpus incoinquinatum*, "when I was better, I came to an uncontaminated body"; *Sirach* (11.12): *plus deficiens uirtute et abundans paupertate*, "more lacking in virtue and afflicted by poverty"; from a more traditional literary context than the Bible, Nemesianus's third-century *Eclogues* (4.72) contains *plus est formosus*, "is more attractive."

There are also cases in which the adverb accompanies the comparative form; this happens as early as in Plautus, *Amphitruo*, 301: *magis . . . maiorem . . . concipiet metum*, literally "he will be afflicted by a more greater fear," and is quite common in Late Latin authors such as Apuleius, in whose *Metamorphosis* (XI.10) we find *ostendebat . . . manum sinistram . . . quae uidebatur aequitati magis aptior quam dextera*, "he showed his left hand, which seemed more suited to justice than his right." This is also found in the Bible, as in Saint Mark's Gospel (5.26): *magis deterius habebat* (although this is translated in the Revised Standard Version as "she rather grew worse"), and *Sirach* (23.28): *oculi Domini multo plus lucidiores super solem*, "the eyes of the Lord are much brighter than the sun."

This evidence shows that there was a tendency in speech to use the explicit comparative adverbs rather than rely on the suffixed forms alone; as we see in the last four examples here, the older forms were tending to become semantically devalued, in that their explicitly comparative meaning may no longer have been generally clear. In any event, the Romance languages have continued the adverbial pattern and lost the suffixes. In Ibero-Romance and in the East, the surviving adverb derives from *magis*; thus the Latin for "more beautiful" was *formosior*, but the Spanish is *más hermoso*, and the Rumanian is *mai frumos*. In the other Romance areas, the surviving adverb derives from *plus*; thus the Latin for "easier" was *facilior*, but the French is *plus facile*, and the Italian is *più facile*. But it is noticeable that the originally irregular comparative and superlative forms were often able to resist this onslaught; thus Spanish *mejor*, French *meilleur*, and Italian *migliore*, all meaning "better," are continuations of the Latin accusative *meliorem*. Other forms of this type also survive as stylistic or semantic alternatives; for example, for "worse," French can use either *pire* (< *peior*) or *plus mauvais* (< *plus malifatius*), and adverbially *pis* (< *peius*) or *plus mal* (< *plus male*); or the originally irregular forms can survive with a specialized meaning, as when *seniorem*, "older," survives as Spanish *señor* and French *seigneur*, originally "gentleman," and *senior* as French *sire* (which was borrowed by English as *sir*).

The superlative suffix did not survive; the Romance equivalent involves the definite article added to the comparative, as in Spanish *más grande*, "larger," and *el más grande*, "the largest," which is a consequence of the invention of this article and its syntax (see section 6.2 below). But it probably disappeared very gradually and at a late date; some of the forms are still in Old French, such as *pesme* from Latin *pessimum*, "worst," and in Spanish, such as *prójimo* from Latin *proximum*, "closest." Italian has subsequently reintroduced *-issimo* as a productive suffix, from the Latin tradition, even in colloquial speech, and formations of this type are now also found in educated speech in other Romance languages.

The simplification of the nominal inflectional system also affected the genders, as has been mentioned in passing already. At the same time as the inflections in use were diminishing, the number of genders was slimming down from three to two. Latin had three genders of noun, known as the masculine, the feminine, and the neuter; the Romance languages now have no more than two, the masculine and the feminine. There are a few fossilized remains of originally neuter forms, but as a separate nominal category, the neuter no longer exists. Vulgar texts offer evidence of the weakening of the neuter category as early as the first century A.D. For example, the neuter nouns *balneum* (bath), *fatum* (destiny), *uas* (dish), and *uinum* (wine) are given a masculine *-us* inflection in Petronius (as *balneus*, *fatus*, *uasus*, and *uinus*). Other kinds of innovation turn up later; neuter plurals ended in *-a*, and when they had a collective meaning, they were often treated as if they were feminine singulars (which also regularly ended in *-a*); thus *folia*, plural of the neuter *folium* (leaves), and *persica*, plural of the neuter *persicum* (peaches), used in texts toward the end of the Empire, have feminine singular descendants in Romance such as, for "leaf," Spanish *hoja*, French *feuille*, and Italian *foglia* (now with separately formed regular feminine plurals in *hojas*, *feuilles*, and *foglie*) and, for "peach," French *pêche* and Italian *pesca*. Some abstract neuter nouns that were regularly used in the plural, for some emphatic purpose, also had the plural form change to feminine singular: Latin *gaudia*, "joys," became French *joie*; Latin *fortia* was the neuter plural of the adjective *fortis*, thus originally meaning "strong things," and came to mean "force" in Spanish *fuerza*, French *force*, and Italian *forza*.

But these changes of gender, from neuter singular to masculine singular and, in several special cases, from neuter plural to feminine singular, do not mean that the loss of the whole neuter gender happened early. In Vulgar texts written during the Empire such uncertainties are still not the norm, and a statistical analysis of such mistakes from the second half of the first millennium shows that, even then, writers and copyists must still have had some kind of vague understanding that the neuter was a different gender from the others. The definitive disappearance of the category can only have happened shortly before the arrival of the first texts in new written Romance form. What is more significant is the noticeable decline, in the Vulgar texts of the Empire, in the syntactic role played by the distinctions between genders, a decline that can only have abetted the reduction of their number. In fact, we can tell that, originally, concord of gender and of number was the explicit bond that united a pronoun to the noun it referred to, particularly in the case of a relative pronoun and its antecedent. This bond seems to have relaxed during the Empire: mistakes in concord became increasingly frequent, and the forms of the relative pronouns, in particular, seem to have become ambiguous as regards gender. Some of the trajectory of this change is clear from mistakes made in texts; the masculine nominative form *qui* (who) and the masculine accusative *quem* came to be generally available forms that could be used after any antecedent, particularly if they were used to refer to people: for example, from the fifth century, *Leucadia deo sacrata puella qui uitam suam prout proposuerat gessit* (CIL XIII 2354), "Leucadia, a girl sacred to God, who lived her life as she had intended," where "who" is rendered by the masculine *qui* rather than the feminine *quae*; or *Clodia cara . . . quem flet . . . coniunx* (CIL VI 15806), "Dear Claudia, who her husband weeps for," with masculine *quem* rather than feminine *quam*. In the *Mulomedicina Chironis*, the supposedly neuter word *iumentum*, "beast of burden," is often accompanied by a masculine relative pronoun, as in *eum iumentum qui* (387).

We can also see a spread in the use of the neuter form *quod*, but this has nothing to do with the fact that it is of neuter gender; *quod* is often used when the antecedent is masculine or feminine, particularly when the nouns are used to refer to abstractions or to objects. This is so in the inscription *memorie . . . q(u)od matrona Nezrifa fecit patri suo* (CIL VIII 21534), "the memorial [tomb?] that the lady Nezrifa made for her father." Cases like this are very common toward the end of the Empire, and even more so after that, and show that the syntactic function of the genders was losing its relevance. It is true that the distinction between masculine and feminine remained (and remains) completely operative, but that is probably due to the partial correspondence of this distinction to the distinction between male and female in the real world, and also, perhaps, to the fact that the system had a stable and increasingly clear phonological opposition between the two, in that in Romance the great majority of feminine nouns ended in [-a] and the great majority of masculine nouns ended in [-o]. In contrast, the neuter was not associated with any particular distinction in the outside world, and its endings coincided for the most part with masculine inflections, so it is understandable that it came to be less useful and less used.

In considering the loss of the inflectional distinctions, we saw that this was made feasible by several developments in the grammar as a whole. We could use similar reasoning as regards the genders: as we shall see, the order of the elements within the sentence was becoming more and more standardized, less free, and these standardized arrangements expressed the grammatical relations between the constituents more clearly than did concord in gender and in number, which in any case involved risky inflections that speakers were unsure about.

The final examples in this section concern pronouns, whose development is more problematic. The most complicated developments seem to have concerned the demonstratives. Two of them, the anaphoric *is* (he, she, it) and the pronoun of identity *idem* (the same), do not survive anywhere in Romance. Only a few traces of *hic* (this) survive: Occitan *oc* continues the neuter form *hoc*; some forms were originally compound, such as French *ce* (this), which comes from *ecce hoc* (this here), and Old French *oïl* (yes), which comes from Latin *hoc ille* ("so he [did, said]"; it later developed phonetically to *oui*); Old Spanish had *agora* (now), from Latin *hac hora* ("at this time," Modern Spanish *ahora*) and *ogaño* (this year), from Latin *hoc anno*. The forms of *ille* (that, near to him) and *iste* (that, near to you) were more tenacious; *ille* survives as the third-person personal pronoun (he, she, it, they), and it is also the starting point for what was to become the Romance definite article (see section 6.2 below). In some Romance areas, *iste*, and also *ipse* (originally "self," "same"), survive; *iste* became *este* in Spain and *ast* in Rumania (this), and *ipse* became Rumanian *îns*, Italian *esso*, Old French *es*, Spanish *ese* (that). In addition, *iste*, like *ille*, also survives as the second half of a compound with *ecce* (or its variant *eccum*): thus *ecce illum* gave Old French *cel* (that), and *ecce istum* gave Old French *cest* (this); *eccum illum* gave Italian *quello*, and *eccum istum* gave Italian *questo*; another variant, *accum*, seems to have been prevalent on the Iberian Peninsula, leading to such forms as Catalan *aquest* and Old Spanish *aqueste* (this).

The developments that led to all this are not well attested in writing. There is a great increase in the use of *ille* and *ipse* after the end of the Empire, true, but the forms of *is*, *hic*, and *idem* continue to be used as well, even in the most "vulgar" of texts. The reinforced forms with *ecce* are found here and there, but are not common. What is more striking, at least in the eyes of a traditional Latinist, is the appearance in late inscriptions, and especially in texts later than the fifth century, of some analogical formations (which happen to be the first signs of later Romance forms). The forms of *ille*, *iste*, and *ipse* are partly changed by analogy with the forms of the relative *qui*. Thus the masculine nominative singular is commonly written in texts of the Merovingian period as *illi*, apparently under the influence of the [-i:] of *qui*, and the existence of the spoken form [illi:] explains how Old French has both *il* and *li* as its masculine singular definite article for the sentence subject. The relative dative singular form, *cui*, served as the model for the analogical creation of the dative *illui* (later to become French and Italian *lui*); the relative genitive singular form, *cuius*, led to a genitive form *illuius*. In the Classical language, the dative singular of both genders was *illi*, but all along there had also existed the form *illae* (and *ipsae* and *istae* as well), created by analogy with the feminine singular dative of nouns such as *terrae*; and then this *illae*, itself an analogical creation, was subsequently reformed yet again by a further analogical process to become *illaei*, analogous with the masculine *illui*; this *illaei* survives in Italian *lei* (she). The genitive plural *illorum* also survived in wide areas of the Romance world, to become (for both genders) French *leur*, Italian *loro*, and Rumanian *-lor*.

2. Verbal Morphology

The first impression that we get from reading Latin texts of a vulgar nature, even the latest and the most incoherent, is that the system of verbal morphology has survived remarkably well. While the nominal morphology of the late and Vulgar texts, particularly after the end of the Empire, is like a ruined city where nothing remains where it originally was, the verbs in the same texts are often found in their usual shape, apart from the fact that some of the spellings reflect phonetic changes (although collectively these are less significant than in the nominal inflections); and the way the verbal inflections are used corresponds, on the whole, to their Classical functions. A quick look at the Romance languages shows us that this first impression can only be an accurate one; the Latin system of nominal morphology hardly survives at all in Romance, but the system of verbal morphology is still rich and full, fuller even than that of Classical Latin, despite the fact that some categories have been lost.

Thus the way in which linguists investigate this topic has to be rather different from the method used in the examination of nominal morphology. In the case of the nouns and adjectives, a study of the relevant texts is enough in itself to show us what was happening; even if we had no information about Romance, we would be able to glimpse the essential features of the gradual emaciation of the nominal system just by looking at the texts. This is not true at all of the verb; it is only by working out what the essential differences are between the Latin and Romance verb systems that we can separate, out of the mass of Vulgar textual symptoms that do not in themselves seem especially significant, those that do indeed correspond to the main lines of evolution in Late Latin from those that do not.

There were four inflectional types (conjugations) of Latin verb. These are usually identified by their infinitival endings. Thus the first conjugation was of the *-are* type, such as *laudare* (praise) and *amare* (love). The second had infinitives ending in *-ere* with a stressed long [é:], such as *habere* (have) and *videre* (see). The third had infinitives ending in *-ere* with a short [e] and the stress on the stem; the "theme" at the end of the stem in these verbs was usually a consonant, such as in *agere* (carry out), which had *ago* as the first-person singular present indicative, but there was also an important subgroup with the theme vowel [i], such as *facere* (do), of which the first-person singular present indicative was *facio*. The fourth conjugation had a theme vowel [i:] and infinitives ending in *-ire*, such as *audire* (hear), which had a first-person singular present indicative in *audio*. In addition, a number of irregular verbs, such as *esse* (be), *ferre* (bring), and *uelle* (want), some of them partially suppletive, did not belong to any of these four types.

Each conjugation of verb had its forms organized into the same categories. The formal categories established by traditional grammar were as follows: three moods, indicative, subjunctive, and imperative; for transitive verbs, two voices, active and passive; six tenses in the indicative—which in the traditional terminology comprise the *infectum* and the *perfectum*, each with past, present, and future, as in *amo* ("I love," present), *amabam* ("I was loving," imperfect), and *amabo* ("I will love," future) for the *infectum*, and *amaui* ("I loved," perfect), *amaueram* ("I had loved," pluperfect), and *amauero* ("I will have loved," future perfect) for the *perfectum*—plus four tenses in the subjunctive (which lacked future or future perfect forms); and, for each paradigm, six person forms, first, second, and third person in both singular and plural. The imperative was a general exception to these, since it had two tenses, present and future, of which the present had second-person singular and second-person plural forms and the future, in addition, had third-person forms. This was a complicated system overall, and it is hardly surprising that already in Classical times there were some uncertainties and several analogical usages; indeed, from this point of view, it is extraordinary that the system's main structural features have survived the centuries, for all these categories are still entirely functional in Romance.

Some verbs moved from one conjugation to another, but the great majority of verbs stayed where they were. It was easy for the third-conjugation verbs with the [i] theme vowel to move, analogically, to the fourth; thus we find the infinitive *fugire* rather than the original *fugere* ("run away," with the normal first-person singular present indicative *fugio*), and the deponent—that is, formally passive but functionally active—infinitive *moriri* for the regular *mori* ("die," with the normal first-person singular *morior*); these new attested forms underlie the Romance developments such as, respectively, Spanish *huir* and *morir*, French *fuir* and *mourir*, and Italian *fuggire* and *morire*, all with stressed [í]. But the greatest movement between conjugations took place between the second and third, in both directions. Thus the third-conjugation infinitive *sapere* (know), originally with unstressed short [e], must have acquired the stressed long [é:] and all the second conjugation's other corresponding inflections, since all Romance languages inherit the second-conjugation forms of this verb—French *savoir* and Italian *sapere* ([sapére]), for example. Moving in the other direction, the original second-conjugation infinitive *respondere* (answer), with stressed long [e:], turns up as a third-conjugation verb, with a short unstressed [e] in the infinitive, in Italian *rispondere*, and this unstressed [e] has gone entirely in French *répondre*. The porousness of the barrier between these two categories led to its complete disappearance in some areas, most notably on the Iberian Peninsula; Spanish and Portuguese have fused the two types into a single Modern conjugation, and verbs from both types now have the stress on the infinitival [é], as in the original second conjugation. Thus Spanish *haber* (have) and *deber* (must) have developed from originally second-conjugation verbs (cp. French *avoir* and *devoir*, all still stressed on the infinitival ending); but also, in the same Modern conjugation as these, in both Spanish and Portuguese, *vender* (sell) and *perder* (lose) come from the Latin third-conjugation infinitival forms *uendere* and *perdere*, with the originally unstressed ending [-ere] (cp. French *vendre* and *perdre*, still stressed on the stem). Indeed, the attractive power of the second conjugation seems to have spread even further than this, because Vulgar Latin saw the creation of regular forms in this category for a number of the commonest irregular verbs; thus the irregular infinitives *posse* (be able) and *uelle* (want) must have given way to spoken forms ending in [ére] (despite being unattested in writing as *potere or *uolere), with the corresponding second-conjugation inflections in other forms, since we find Old French *pooir* (Modern *pouvoir*), French *vouloir*, and Italian *potere* and *volere*. The second and third conjugations also seem to have amalgamated in Sardinia, but the present Sardinian forms show that in this case they all became third-conjugation verbs with infinitives in unstressed [e]; thus Latin *mouere* ("move," in [-ére]) has become Sardinian *moere*, with stress on the [ó].

Despite these movements between conjugations, even the most important developments in verb morphology did not succeed in changing the essential nature of the system. The first such modification we shall consider was an innovation that did not change the general pattern of the conjugation system at all, but is even so one of the most noticeable developments to have affected verbal morphology: the replacement of the original future tense by periphrastic forms.

The Latin future-tense forms were in some danger from phonetic developments. The future tenses of the first and second conjugations ended in *-bo*, *-bis*, and *-bit* in the singular, and in all the regular first-conjugation verbs the third-person singular form, which is the most frequent and important, came to sound the same as the preterite because the intervocalic [-b-] became fricative; perhaps from the first century onward, the phonetic difference between the future form spelled *laudabit* (he will praise) and the preterite form spelled *laudauit* (he praised) was hard to perceive or even absent. In the third conjugation, where the third-person singular of the future of *agere* was *aget* (he will carry out), the phonetic merger of unstressed [i] and [e] in final syllables, which spread to more and more forms as a consequence of the confusion between the second and third conjugations, meant that often no distinction between the future and the present forms such as *agit* (he carries out) was perceptible.

Here we find the main reason for the occasional uncertainty, attested in Vulgar texts, concerning the use of the future. The symptom of this uncertainty is often the use of a present-tense form with future meaning. This is not in itself totally new, however, since the present was often available anyway to refer to something that was going to happen very soon, in particular if the sentence also included a precise temporal expression that made the futurity unambiguous: thus Cicero, in his *Epistulae ad Atticum* (14.11), wrote *cras mane uadit*, "he goes tomorrow morning," with the verb in the present tense. This use of the present tense with future reference is common in the later texts: thus Egeria, in her *Itinerarium* (12.3), wrote *si uultis uidere loca . . . attendite et uidete, et dicimus uobis*, "if you want to see these places . . . pay attention and watch, and we tell you" (meaning "we will tell you about them").

No less frequent, however, is the replacement of the future form with a periphrasis, and this becomes increasingly common over time. Some periphrastic verbal expressions with a modal auxiliary and an infinitive, such as *facere debeo* (I must do), *facere uolo* (I want to do), had been in existence all along; these modal verbs were in the present tense, but their meaning looked to the future, and it was thus natural that they could be exploited for a simple temporal reference. Even so, they would have brought into that temporal reference an additional modal (and thus subjective) nuance. This probably explains why the commonest periphrasis to be used instead of the simple future in the late texts was the combination of the future participle, ending in *-turus*, and *esse*, "to be"; any modal value that this combination contained was weaker, less explicit, and less noticeable than a periphrasis with *uolo* or *debeo*. So *facturus sum* (I am about to do) came to be a synonymous alternative to *faciam* (I will do).

Among the other periphrases available to speakers, however, one was destined to succeed and survive: the combination of the infinitive with an inflected form of *habere* (have). To begin with, this kind of future periphrasis was not the most frequent, for the most part only used with verbs such as *dicere* (say), *scribere* (write), and *quaerere* (ask). The combination meant something like "have something to say," "have something to write," "have something to ask": thus in Aulus Gellius's *Noctes Atticae* (20.10.2) we find *si quid . . . quaerere habes, quaeras licet*, meaning "if you have something to ask, you can ask it." After the Classical period, this periphrasis was mostly used to express obligation or necessity; so *facere habeo* then meant "I must do." This periphrasis gets relatively commoner in the writings of the Church Fathers, though it is even then less frequently used than the others mentioned above; but from the first it seems that it was possible to use it without any particular modal meaning at all, referring straightforwardly just to the future. For example, where the Vulgate version of Saint John's Gospel (8.22) gives us *Numquid interficiet semetipsum* (Will he kill himself?), a manuscript of the Itala, the old biblical translation (which was revised by Saint Jerome for the Vulgate), reads *occidere se habet*. We find the same construction, but with a past-tense form of *habere*, in one of the Itala manuscripts' versions of Saint Luke (19.4); here *habebat transire* was changed by Saint Jerome to *erat transiturus*, in the sentence *ascendit in arborem . . . ut uideret eum, quia inde erat transiturus* ("so he ran on ahead and climbed up into a sycamore tree to see him, for he was to pass that way," in the Revised Standard Version). Presumably this way of expressing the future became common first in the contexts to which it was most suited; it is noticeable that Tertullian, one of the first authors to adopt this periphrasis at all frequently, apart from the anonymous biblical translators, usually uses it with a past-tense form of *habere* and a passive infinitive: thus in his *Aduersus Marcionem* (4.8) we read *Nazareus uocari habebat secundum prophetiam*, "he was to be called the Nazarene, according to the prophecy." This combination, with the present-tense forms of *habere* following the active infinitive, is what underlies the future tense in all the main Romance languages, apart from Rumanian, which still uses periphrases; thus from Latin *cantare habeo* (I have to sing) come French *chanterai*, Spanish *cantaré*, and Italian *canterò*, all meaning "I will sing." With the imperfect (in Italian, with the perfect) of *habere*, this periphrasis was the basis of forms that refer to the future as seen from the past, and that function, furthermore, as the present of the conditional mood, a specifically Romance category that did not exist in Latin—such as Spanish *cantaría* from Latin *cantare habebam*, meaning "I would sing," "I was going to sing."

One explanation that Romance linguists have suggested for the success of this periphrasis with *habere* has been based on its original modal value, in that the idea of futurity is essentially linked in the speaker's subconscious with the emotional attitudes expressed by *habere*; that is, the future is typically the object of intentions, desires, and fears. Probably, though, the exact opposite is the true reason; of all the available periphrases formed with an infinitive and an auxiliary, the one involving *habere* was the least subjectively modal and the most objective. In addition, the combination of the infinitive with *habere* had the advantage of greater flexibility than the periphrasis with *-turus sum*, since *-turus* could not be used in the passive voice; it also had simpler phonetics, since *habere* began with a vowel (the *h-* was silent by the time in question), and several of its forms were monosyllables, such as [as] (written as *habes* still, of course, and never as **-as*), or simple disyllables, such as [ajo] (still written *habeo*). This meant that it was quite a straightforward matter to turn these forms into the inflections of a new synthetic (that is, one-word) paradigm. The first written form reflecting this new future inflectional system appears in the seventh-century historical compilation traditionally bearing the name of a fictitious author, Fredegarius or Fredegar, in which (II.62) the author explains the name of the city Daras through a play on words: the emperor Justinian, negotiating with the defeated king of Persia, is said to have replied *daras* (that is, "you will give," as in Modern Spanish *darás*, from *dare habes*) when the king refused to give up the conquered areas.

As noted at the start, the change in the nature of the future does not affect the general structural pattern of the verb system; Latin had a synthetic future indicative and so does Romance, and in this respect the system of temporal contrasts between the tenses is identical in the two.

Something very similar happened in the replacement of the Latin passive voice by another kind of passive, with the difference that the use of the passive is considerably less frequent in Romance than it had been in Latin. This is not, of course, a difference in the grammar. In the Latin passive voice, the present, imperfect, and future tenses of every active verb had a synthetic passive counterpart; thus *amo* (I love), *amor* (I am loved); *amabam* (I was loving), *amabar* (I was being loved); *amabo* (I will love), *amabor* (I will be loved). In the perfect, pluperfect, and future perfect tenses, the passive was created by periphrases made up of the past participle and the relevant form of *esse* (to be): thus *amaui* (I loved), *amatus sum* (I was loved); *amaueram* (I had loved), *amatus eram* (I had been loved); *amauero* (I will have loved), *amatus ero* (I will have been loved). What happened in Romance was that the system became completely analytical; every surviving passive form is periphrastic, and the old synthetic passive forms of the present, imperfect, and future have not survived anywhere in Romance, even in the earliest attested texts. In most Romance languages, these were replaced by the periphrases with the participle and *esse*; that is, to present it from another perspective, the combination of past participle and *esse* underwent a semantic change and lost its past meaning, such that the tense of the compound came to be that explicitly represented in the form of *esse*. In this way *amatus sum* changed from meaning "I was loved" to mean "I am loved" (the meaning hitherto expressed by *amor*), and *amatus eram* changed its meaning from "I had been loved" to "I was loved" (hitherto expressed by *amabar*). This is why the French present passive is *je suis aimé* and the Spanish *soy amado*, and the imperfect passives are respectively *j'étais aimé* and *era amado*. A consequence of this development was that the original meanings of *amatus sum* and *amatus eram*, etc., had to be expressed by combinations that were alien to Classical Latin grammar, such as *amatus fui* for "I was loved" and *amatus fueram* for "I had been loved," whence French *je fus aimé* and Spanish *fui amado*, with the tense explicitly and only marked in the auxiliary.

So we know the starting and ending points of this development, the Latin and Romance passive systems, but the evolutionary process that led from the one to the other is not at all easy to reconstruct. The texts, even the latest and most "vulgar" ones, such as the Merovingian diplomas, still used the Classical passive system and usually presented the original synthetic forms with their original meanings. But if we look more closely at these, we get the impression that the survival of the synthetic passive, although neither totally artificial nor absent from speech, was restricted even so to certain expressions, certain verbs, certain forms, and even a certain style. For example, we often see a passive infinitive used in a Merovingian text where the active might have been ambiguous; that is, the passive is here introduced from a literary desire for clarity. Thus Gregory of Tours, for example, in his *Historia Francorum* (IV.5), writes: *ut uiuens plebem suam uastari non cerneret*, "so that he would not in his lifetime see his people being devastated" (where the active infinitive *uastare* would be understood as seeing the people "devastating" somebody else). We also see a great number of uses of *uidetur* and *uidentur* ("is/are seen"; "seem"), whose usage allows the creation of periphrases that sound official, or legalese, as in the *Concilium Vasense* of the year 529, canon 1, where *in domo ubi ipsi habitare uidentur* just means "in the house where they live," rather than where they "seem to live" (and in addition, the presence of *uidetur* or *uidentur* creates a desirable rhythmic cadence for the end of the sentence). But these come into the category of more or less fixed phrases, which almost certainly still existed in speech, or at least in speech with pretensions to formality, but which were gradually giving way in spontaneous utterances to the new, simpler and clearer two-word passive formations.

The existence of the new kind of passive (with its tense specified in the auxiliary, as in *amatus sum*) is first attested with the new preterite and pluperfect forms that were contrary to the precepts of Classical grammar, such as the indicatives *amatus fui*, *amatus fueram*, and their subjunctive counterparts. These constructions can be found quite commonly in some of the lesser writers of the later years of the Empire; for example, Lucifer of Cagliari, in his *De non conueniendo cum haereticis*, VIII, wrote *metuentes . . . ne illa fuissent dicta de illis*, meaning "fearing . . . that those things had been said about them." It is possible that the change in the passive system did in fact begin here, in the use of these new forms in which a perfect or pluperfect tense in the auxiliary *esse* explicitly signaled the perfect or pluperfect meaning, and that subsequently the presence of *amatus fui*, for example, with past meaning, was the catalyst that allowed *amatus sum* to promote itself definitively to the present tense. Thereupon, in the ensuing rivalry to express "I am loved" between the old synthetic present form *amor* and the new analytic form *amatus sum*, the older form was probably doomed. This latter development would have been abetted by the presence of deponent verbs; these were verbs active in meaning but passive in form, such as *loquor* (speak) and *sequor* (follow), and in speech the forms of these verbs seem naturally to have led to all sorts of confusions and inconsistencies of usage, as well as insecurities among the less-educated over which were the traditionally correct forms of the passive.

Romance contains one other basic innovation compared with Latin: the so-called compound tenses. These are tense forms that combine the past participle with an auxiliary, usually that descending from *habere*. In some languages, including French, the auxiliary can in some circumstances be the descendant of *esse* as well. These compound tenses carry out the same functions as synthetic tense forms, and their arrival compensated to a large extent for the loss of some of these (see below). They were early in origin: the combination of *habere* and the past participle was already used in Classical times; but the Romance development is semantically different. Originally, in such combinations, *habere* kept its full lexical meaning of "possess," "hold," "have in one's control," and the participle was used to refer to an action carried out by the agent subject of both verbs: thus in Livy (22.4.5), for example, *ubi clausum lacu ac montibus et circumfusum suis copiis habuit hostem*, "when he had the enemy in his power, shut in by the lake and the mountains and surrounded by his own troops." Sometimes, however, the action referred to with the participle was mental rather than tangible or physical, such that the combination of the two verbs was not obviously used to refer to two separate activities and the verbs were thus felt to be more closely united: thus we find in Cicero's *Epistulae ad familiares* (13.17.3), for example, *sin autem . . . nondum eum satis habes cognitum*, "but if you still haven't got him sufficiently known," where the reference is the same as in the immediately preceding clause (13.17.2) *quem si tu iam . . . cognosti*, with a perfect, "if you've already found out about him"; that is, *habes cognitum* means the same as *cognosti* here. This remained the case for a long time, with the periphrasis being used rarely, being neither fixed in form nor grammaticalized.

It is only in texts of the second half of the first millennium that more examples appear, going beyond the traditional cases of the type *cognitum habere* and *compertum habere* (both "to have found out"). When we read in Gregory of Tours's *Historia Francorum* (V.25), for example, *Scis enim quod foedus inter nos initum habemus*, the temptation is to translate it as a normal perfect tense—"Know, then, that we have drawn up a pact between us"—although it could also be taken to mean "we possess a pact that has been drawn up," maintaining the full lexical sense of *habemus*. But there cannot be much doubt about the essential unity of the two parts of the periphrasis when the same author, in his *Vitae patrum* (III.1), writes *Ecce episcopum . . . inuitatum habes, et uix nobis supersunt quattuor uini amphorae* (Look, you've invited the bishop . . . and there are hardly four jugs of wine left). But in this period the construction is neither systematic nor stable; and we should also notice that the order of the two elements is the reverse of the order that turns up in Romance, where *habere* nearly always precedes the participle (for example, this would be *has invitado* in Spanish). In any event, of course, it is likely that the development of such a system of compound verbs would have been more advanced in speech than the texts lead us to suppose. Indeed, it is noticeable that most of the examples that we find in Gregory of Tours are in direct speech, where the author is reproducing the words of actual speakers. Another suggestive piece of evidence is that the majority of the examples, unlike the two quoted above, in fact have a past tense of *habere*, often in the subjunctive, as in Gregory of Tours's (*Historia Francorum*, VI.43) *Audica, qui sororem eius disponsatam habebat, cum exercitu uenit* (Audica, who had married the other man's sister, came with an army). It just seems, then, that the compound forms were available as a more straightforward alternative to some of the original synthetic forms, especially for expressing pluperfect meaning, and also that they seemed particularly useful as alternatives to synthetic subjunctives, as in Gregory of Tours's (*Historia Francorum*, III.27) *cum iam septimus annus esset, quod Wisigardem disponsatam haberet* (since it was now the seventh year after he had married Wisigard).

Vulgar Latin texts can also show us the origins of the periphrasis with *esse* and the past participle for the perfect tense of intransitive verbs. This may at first have been modeled on the analogy of the deponent (and semideponent) verbs whose past participle was accompanied by *esse* anyway, often with perfect meaning, as in *locutus sum* from the deponent *loquor* (I have spoken) and *gauisus sum* from the semideponent *gaudeo* (I have rejoiced); thus we sometimes find *uentus sum*, for "I have come," rather than the original *ueni*, and *processus sum*, "I have gone ahead," rather than *processi*.

The emergence of this system of compounds, used alongside the earlier synthetic forms, almost certainly has something to do with the loss of some forms from the original system, since some parts of the new system could then be used instead of old forms whose use was beginning to seem problematic. The texts from Merovingian Gaul, for example, are full of word forms that seem to have confused the imperfect subjunctive (e.g., *amarem, caperem*) with the perfect subjunctive (in these cases, *amauerim, ceperim*). This confusion was both phonetic and functional; for example, in the historical compilation said to be by Fredegar (IV.72) we find *petentes ut eos in terra Francorum . . . receperit*, "asking him to take them into the land of the Franks," where the meaning, which is looking to the future rather than to the past, seems to require *reciperet* instead. The perfect subjunctive was anyway, in most persons, identical with the future perfect indicative (for example, both were *amaueris* in the second-person singular); and then the loss of intervocalic [w] (spelled -*u*-) led both these to sound very similar to the second-person singular present passive form *amaris*, which, as we have seen, was in trouble itself already; so it can be seen that the forms whose endings were based on -*r*- were experiencing difficulties in speech. These forms included the pluperfect indicative active (*amaueram*, etc.), the future perfect indicative active (*amauero*, etc.), the imperfect subjunctive active (*amarem*, etc.) and the perfect subjunctive (*amauerim*, etc.). Large numbers of these have gone from much of Romance, but their disappearance was gradual, late, and patchy. Sardinian still has a subjunctive deriving from *amarem*, for example. The Oldest French to be attested retained the original pluperfect indicative forms, but with simple past meaning, such as *auret* (from *habuerat*) and others from the *Sequence of Saint Eulalia*, and so did Old Occitan. In Spanish the form of this synthetic pluperfect also survives, although it now has the value of an imperfect subjunctive (*amauerat* > *amara*, *legerat*, "had read" > *leyera*); in Portuguese it is still an indicative. Old Spanish had a future subjunctive form that seems to have derived from both the original perfect subjunctive and the future perfect, *cantare* < *cantauerit*; Modern Spanish legalese still does. That these problems were probably phonetic in origin can be seen from the fact that the original pluperfect subjunctive forms (such as *amauissem*, which is phonetically quite distinct from any other finite form) survive cheerfully all over the Romance world.

There are no developments worth mentioning in the rest of the verbal inflection system, apart from the usual phonetic changes. We know, for example, from the grammarian Probus, who condemned this pronunciation (GL, IV.160), and from epigraphic evidence, that the *perfectum* forms, particularly of the verbs ending in *-are*, had contracted forms in speech, such as seem to be attested by the forms *probai*, for *probaui* (I tried), and *probait*, *probaut*, and even *probat*, for *probauit* (he tried). This is valuable evidence, since Romance forms such as French *prouvai* and *prouva*, Spanish *probé* and *probó*, are explained on the basis of these spoken usages.

The Latin system had a large number of nonfinite forms. The Vulgar texts do not allow us to glimpse much change here, but Romance has lost several of them. The perfect infinitives, such as *amauisse* (to have loved), do not survive at all, despite the survival of the pluperfect subjunctives, such as *amauissem*, which shows that the reason for their loss cannot have been simply phonetic. The future participles ending in *-turus* have also gone. The past participles have survived, although several have undergone analogical remodeling; the most important case involved the spread of a form ending in *-utus*, with stressed [u]. There were only a handful of such participles in Latin, including *secutus* from *sequor* (follow), *fututus* from *futuo* (have sex with), and *consutus* from *consuo* (stitch); yet this replaced the unstressed participial ending in several verbs, such as *habere*, where it is an unattested form with [u], *habutum, rather than the original *habitum*, which underlies Italian *avuto*, Rumanian *avut*, and Old French *eü*; similarly, *credutum rather than *creditum* underlies Italian *creduto*, Rumanian *crezut*, and Old French *creü*. Ibero-Romance began to go the same way, with a number of Old Spanish participles ending in *-udo*, but none of these have survived into the Modern language.

6

PHRASES AND SENTENCES

It would take too long to present even a bird's-eye view of all the syntactic phenomena found in Vulgar Latin; the discussion will here confine itself instead to an account of the most characteristic phenomena. I have in any event mentioned several syntactic matters while describing the morphological developments and their contexts in the previous chapter.

1. Noun Phrases

Noun phrases, the groups of words containing nouns and their companions (such as determiners, adjectives, possessives, and nouns in apposition), seem to have undergone several unspectacular but basic changes in Late Vulgar Latin. The most noticeable change concerns the very gradual move toward a more fixed word order for the internal components of the noun phrase. To be more precise about this evolutionary process, we would need to have at our disposal statistical evidence that we have not yet managed to get; and unfortunately, even though new studies are produced on this topic all the time, our understanding of Late Latin word order is still fragmentary.

We can be sure of a few points, however. In the first place, the increasing fixedness of word order was accompanied by a greater internal cohesion of the phrase. If we consider phrases containing an adjective of any kind and a noun, we can state one development with certainty. It is common in Classical prose texts—my own rough calculations suggest that it happens about one time in three in Caesar, and one time in five or six in the philosophical works of Cicero—that some other element comes between an adjective and the noun to which it is allied; this can either be an element from outside the phrase entirely or one that is tied to the noun in some other way. For example, in Cicero's *De Amicitia* (IX.29)—*quibus rebus ad illum primum motum animi et amoris adhibitis, admirabilis quaedam exardescit beneuolentiae magnitudo*, "when all of this is added to the first movement of feeling and love, there will be the flame of an admirably strong attraction"—not only the possessive genitive *beneuolentiae*, but also the verb itself, *exardescit*, separates the adjective *admirabilis* from its noun, *magnitudo*. Separating an adjective from its noun like this is very unusual in the late texts, and even when it does happen, it seems to be a more or less fixed formula or a literary echo. For an example, consider this section from the treatise on diet by the physician Anthimus (chapter 21): *De ficato porcino frixo penitus non expedit nec sanis nec infirmis. Sani tamen, si uolunt, sic manducent: . . . in graticula ferrea, quae habet latas uirgas . . . in subtilis carbonis assent ita, ut crudastros sint.* "As regards fried pig's liver, this is not to be recommended, neither for the healthy nor for the ill. Healthy people can, however, if they wish, eat it like this: it should be fried on an iron grill with wide bars over a slow coal fire, so that it still stays fairly raw." In this case, and in almost all other relevant cases in Anthimus's text, the adjectives come next to the nouns they are allied to. The few cases in this text where the two are separated are almost all a kind of formula that reappears at the heads of sections, such as *de carnibus uero uaccinis* (chapter 3, "about calf meat"), *uerbicinas uero carnis* (chapter 4, "about ram meat"), *agnelinas uere carnis* (chapter 5, "about lamb meat"); here *carnis*, "meat," is an alternative form of the accusative plural *carnes*. Thus, apart from a few odd exceptions, noun and adjective in this text form a united phrase.

The same kind of development can be seen in the case of a noun and its possessive (in the genitive case). In the Classical language it was quite common to separate these two, but in Vulgar texts it hardly happens at all. So it seems that in speech, which would have gone much further in this direction than the texts (which always have some echo of the Classical language), it was becoming normal for the component parts of a noun phrase to be contiguous.

The fixing of a normal order for the elements within a noun phrase, though, happened much more slowly than the establishment of contiguity, particularly as regards the order of adjective and noun. From a grammatical point of view, either order was possible in Classical Latin, and this remained the case in Late Latin too. Indeed, it is often still the case in Romance that either order is acceptable. In Vulgar texts it is just as common to find the adjective first as it is to find the noun first, and the only hard rule is their contiguity. It is highly likely, of course, that in context the choice of one position or the other for the adjective was made on stylistic or pragmatic grounds, but it is unfortunately not usually practical now to try to state these reasons with the necessary clarity. It is easier for us to see what was happening as regards the relative order of noun and possessive genitive; in Classical texts, it is only marginally less common to have the genitive preposed than postposed, but in texts of a more "vulgar" character the genitive is nearly always second. In Gregory of Tours's *Historia Francorum*, for example, if the genitive comes first, this marks it as carrying some kind of emphasis: thus (III.7) *eamus cum Dei adiutorio contra eos*, "let's go against them with the help of God," is emphasizing "God," although at times this order just seems to be the result of a pedantic literary pomposity, as in (III.9) *uellim umquam Aruernam Lemanem, quae tantae iocunditatis gratia refulgere dicitur, oculis cernere*, "I would like some time to see with my own eyes Limagne, in the Auvergne, which is said to shine with the grace of very great beauty." In passages where the tone of the description is more natural, the genitive is nearly always postposed, as it is in the three cases in (III.7): *Theudoricus non immemor periurias Hermenefredi regis . . . aduersum eum ire disponit, promittens regi Chlothachario partem praedae, si eisdem munus uicturiae diuinitus conferritur*, "Theudoricus has not forgotten the perjuries of King Hermenefred . . . prepares to march against him, promising a part of the booty to King Chlothacharius, if God grants them the gift of victory."

Fixing the position of the constituent parts of the noun phrase in this way is one symptom of a wider change in the nature of the grammar, a change that is indeed one of the most far-reaching in the transition from Latin to Romance. From Late Latin texts onward, it is not so much the morphological inflections at the ends of the constituent words, as the positions in which they appear, that signal the grammatical relationships between the elements of the same noun phrase. Henceforth within a noun phrase cohesion between a noun and an adjective is guaranteed by their *juxtaposition*; a noun can be understood as being determinant of another (for instance, in a possessive relation) by its mere *postposition*. The decreasing syntactic relevance of the morphological inflections is also made entirely clear by the growing lack of precise concord between the elements in the same noun phrase. More and more we notice the use of a nominative inflection in an adjective or in a noun in apposition, which should strictly have the same inflection as the noun to which it is allied; for example (*CIL* VIII 15797), *curantibus filis Saturus et Muthun*, which is an ablative absolute clause meaning "with his sons Saturus and Muthun organizing the funeral," contains the nominative *Saturus* rather than the ablative *Saturo*; similarly, in (*CIL* VIII 22570) *C. Aurelio Valerio Diocletiano pio felix inuictus*, "to C. Aurelius Valerius Diocletianus, pious, happy, undefeated," we might have expected the datives *felici* and *inuicto*. Most failures to produce proper concord in this way can be called "barbarisms" or "signs of ignorance of correct Latin" from a schoolbook perspective only; linguists realize that the large number of such cases testifies to a redefinition of the relative value of the grammatical features concerned: that is, a loss in the importance, and indeed in the existence, of some of the inflections and of paradigmatic features in general, and a concomitant increase in the importance of distributional features (the position of the elements in relation to each other).

We should also note the growing frequency, particularly in texts written after the end of the Empire, of the use of the demonstrative pronouns, mainly *ipse* (originally "same") and *ille* (originally "that"), as adjectives. We can see both used this way in Theodosius's *De situ terrae sanctae* (20): *Memoria sancti Helysei ubi fontem illum benedixit ibi est et super ipsa memoria ecclesia fabricata est*, "That's where the tomb of Saint Elysius is, where he blessed that spring, and a church has been built on the same tomb." This usage is very common in legal and official documents. We can see it in, for example, Fredegar (IV.45): *anno* XXXIV *regni Chlothariae legatus tres nobilis ex gente Langobardorum . . . ad Clothario destinantur, petentes, ut illa duodece milia soledorum, quas annis singulis Francorum aerariis dissoluebant, debuissent cassare,* "in the thirty-fourth year of Clotharius's reign, three noble emissaries from the Lombard people were sent to Clotharius asking him to release them from paying the twelve thousand solidi that they paid to the Frankish treasury each year." Constructions of this kind were eventually going to lead to the definite articles of Romance, but it would be wrong to describe these demonstratives as already being articles; their usage does not yet have the automatic and grammaticalized character of the article, and they still usually have a recognizably anaphoric function, referring back to previously mentioned entities: in the first example here, the phrase *fontem illum* means "that spring which you already know about," and *ipsa memoria* similarly means "the tomb in question"; and in the second, the phrase *illa duodece milia soledorum* is still interpretable with a demonstrative value ("those twelve thousand solidi").

2. The Simple Sentence

I have already mentioned in previous chapters a number of problems concerning sentence structure, and only a few basic questions will be considered here, particularly the question of word order within the sentence. In this respect, the Vulgar evidence does not suggest that there was a great change from the Classical tendencies. In texts of all kinds we find all the six possible orders of subject (S), verb (V), and direct or indirect object or prepositional phrase (O), including SVO but also SOV, VSO, and the others. Any more complicated order can be created by the inclusion of further complements or subordinate clauses, which can separate these three from each other; and, of course, many sentences lack a subject or an object or both. This is the case in Classical texts, and it is also the case in Late and Vulgar Latin texts. It is, perhaps, rather surprising to see the contrast between the increasingly fixed order within the noun phrase and this continuing freedom of word order at the sentence level during the same period, but there is a good reason for the survival of this freedom: it was still possible to distinguish subject from object without relying on the word order, even after the start of the decline in use of the nominal inflections. The nominative and the accusative inflections indicated the subject and direct object respectively, and (as we saw above) in most cases their forms remained distinct throughout the Late Latin period and thus recognizable whatever their position in the sentence; and the other inflections were replaced by prepositional phrases that could equally intelligibly turn up anywhere within the sentence.

Thus all the possible orders of verb, subject, and object remained grammatically possible and acceptable in Vulgar Latin. Even so, it is true that the statistics concerning their relative frequency change over the years. Classical Latin, particularly in the highest-style literary registers, seems to have favored placement of the verb at the end. Authors did this deliberately, thinking it particularly appropriate to such a style. Indeed, Caesar puts the verb last in 80 to 90 percent of his clauses; in two-thirds of the clauses that contain a subject at all, the subject is first and the verb is last, whatever else is there, as, for example, in his *De bello civili* (I.16): *Caesar legionibus traductis ad oppidum constitit*, "Caesar, after the legions had been taken over the river, stopped outside the town." Taking these facts into account, Latin has been considered from the typological point of view—based on the order of the essential syntactic elements in the sentence—an SOV-type language. But this categorization of the language as basically having SOV order is exaggerated, even as regards the Classical language; we can tell that in other genres of a less-elevated nature than historiography, such as in Cicero's *Dialogues*, for example, the statistics are not the same as in Caesar; here, verb-final sentences are not the dominant type. In late texts verb-final sentences are still common but also less than a majority; in most texts that we might wish to characterize as "vulgar" the proportion of verb-final sentences is 50 percent at most. Statistically, the characteristic feature of Late Latin texts seems to be to have the verb between the two noun phrases if two are there (including prepositional phrases)—that is, either SVO or OVS. Both these orders seem to have gained ground statistically since Classical times, and in some texts they form the clear majority. For example, Antoninus of Placentia, in the second half of the sixth century, writes, in his *Itinerarium* (5), *in sinagoga posita est trabis*, "in the synagogue is placed a beam" (OVS), and then (6) *uenimus in Tabor monte, qui mons exurgit in medio campestre*, "we came to Mount Tabor, which mountain rises up in the middle of the plain" (SVO); the order of the elements found in both these sentences is that which was later to come to sound the most natural in Romance.

In questions, meanwhile, there is no noticeable systematic change at all in the order of the constituents; the Vulgar language in this respect was the same as the Classical.

3. Compound Sentences

Naturally, Vulgar Latin did not use the lengthy, complex, and carefully constructed sentences found in literary language; in Vulgar usage the constructions were comparatively simple and straightforward. Vulgar Latin continued using the usual techniques of coordination and subordination, of course, but it reduced the number of conjunctions and relative words that were available to combine sentences into a single unit.

Coordination essentially remained as it always had been, with only slight changes. It is worth mentioning, though, the increasing use of sic (originally "thus") as a coordinating conjunction; thus Egeria, in her *Itinerarium* (43.6), wrote *benedicuntur cathecumini sic fideles*, "the trainees and the faithful were blessed." Some Romance developments go back to this use of *sic*, such as Rumanian și, which means "and"; in Old French (but not Modern French) *si* could also be used in the same way, as in the *Chanson de Roland* (647–48): *Marsilies tint Guenelun par l'espalle. Si li ad dit . . .* "Marsilion's hand on Guènes' shoulder lies; He says to him . . ." (in Dorothy Sayers's translation).

The technique of subordination saw one structural change, but this was an important one; subordinate clauses containing finite verbs were extended for use after main verbs that in the Classical language usually required subordinate clauses containing infinitives. As is well known, after some verbs, particularly verbs of saying and perceiving, Classical literary Latin used the "accusative and infinitive construction," in which the subordinated verb appeared in the infinitive form and its subject was given the accusative inflection (rather than the nominative, which it would have had if the sentence were not subordinated). A sentence such as *patrem aduenisse scio*, meaning "I know that my father has come," would serve as a simple example of this construction: here, *patrem* is accusative and *aduenisse* is the perfect infinitive, literally meaning "I know my father to have come." But there are isolated examples, even from the earliest literary texts, in which the subordinate clause is not of this "accusative and infinitive" type, but instead contains a finite verb introduced by a subordinating conjunction: Plautus's *Asinaria* (52–53), for example, reads *scio iam filius quod amet meus istanc meretricem*, "I already realize that my son loves this prostitute." These are sporadic attestations, however, and it is only in post-Classical texts that examples of this construction become at all common. Then it is found particularly in the Christian authors: the first texts to contain a large number of these constructions are the early biblical translations. Subsequently, in the latest period of the Empire, Vulgar Latin texts of other types use them frequently.

The new construction may have been less concise and less tightly organized than the traditional one, but it can never have been absent from Latin speech; and it also had the advantage of being clearer, more like the syntax of other constructions in its structure and word order, and in practice less likely to lead to ambiguity. For example, the sentence from the *Asinaria* quoted above would have been ambiguous as *filium amare meretricem*, since then both nouns would have been in the accusative and the listeners would not have been sure who was in love with whom. So it is understandable that the construction with the explicit subordinating conjunction should have gradually gained ground, particularly among Christian writers, once its common use in the Latin Bible translations had given it more prestige.

The subordinating conjunctions that came to be used in such cases, after verbs of saying and perceiving, were mainly *quod* and *quia* (as "that"); although *quoniam* (originally "since"), *quomodo* (originally "how"), and even *eo quod* (originally "for the reason which") are also found. The choice of *quod* is unsurprising, since *quod* was almost always the conjunction used in the early examples (such as those found in Plautus), and it was in any event becoming an all-purpose conjunction, as we shall see below. The use of *quia*, which originally meant "because," could well be attributable to Greek influence, since Greek ὅτι (in conformity with the more permissive syntax of Greek in these sentences) could, while being a causal conjunction, also introduce subordinate clauses after verbs of saying and perceiving, where Classical Latin would have needed an "accusative and infinitive" construction; this usage was not exclusively a Grecism, but the analogy with the Greek usage certainly contributed to its increasing frequency. The other conjunctions used in such cases appeared later; these could at times also be explained by analogy, since they too are causal, like *quia*, but they may just have arisen from an authorial desire for variation. Thus in the *Vetus Latina*'s translation of *Genesis* (39.3), we read *Uidit autem dominus eius quod esset Dominus cum eo*, "His master saw that the Lord was with him," where the Greek original had ὅτι; later, Saint Jerome, in the Vulgate, was to go back to more traditional syntax and write *nouerat esse Dominum cum eo* (although in other cases he was happy to use the conjunction, as in the *Vetus Latina*). Other examples include, from the *Mulomedicina Chironis* (59), *scias quod . . . incipiet uulnus pusillum incurabile esse* (with *quod*, "you should know . . . that a little wound will begin to become incurable"); from Saint Ambrose's *De excessu fratris* (1.65.1), *an nescis, quia exemplum tuum periculum ceterorum est?* (with *quia*, "or don't you know that your example is a danger to the others?"); from the fifth-century writer Victor Vitensis (II.25), *dicite quoniam episcopi uobiscum concumbunt et clerici uestri* (with *quoniam*, "admit that your bishops and clerics are going to bed with you"); from the probably fifth-century writer Caelius Aurelianius (II.181), *responderunt . . . quomodo similis arteriarum cordis est motus* (with *quomodo*, "they replied . . . how the movement of the arteries in the heart is similar"; *how* is often used this way in English too); and from the *Liber Pontificalis* (XXII, a chapter probably written in the mid-sixth century), *audiuit Decius eo quod epistolam accepisset a beato Cypriano* (with *eo quod*, "Decius then heard that he had received a letter from St Cyprian," in Raymond Davis's translation).

It is mainly after the end of the Empire that this replacement of the accusative and infinitive by the conjunction and the finite verb, after verbs of saying and perceiving, becomes dominant. The ratio in third- and fourth-century writers is of ten "accusative and infinitive" constructions for every one involving a conjunction and a finite verb; after A.D. 500, the Vulgar writers present a majority of constructions with the conjunction. This development was probably aided by the general reorganization of word order; in all the examples that we have included, for example, the subordinate clause follows the verb of saying or perceiving rather than preceding it. The "accusative and infinitive" clause, on the other hand, could equally come before or after the verb that governed it, and this flexibility helped the construction survive for a long time alongside the rival construction with the conjunction; but the subordinate clause introduced by *quod* or *quia*, on the other hand, very nearly always came after the main verb (except in literary styles where great emphasis was required). So the extension of the sentence pattern in which the verb was no longer normally final but could unremarkably be followed by, for example, a complement subordinate clause was a most helpful factor in the spread of these subordinate clauses with *quod*.

This construction was to lead to the one found in most of Romance, where verbs of saying and perceiving are usually followed by the subordinating conjunction (such as French and Spanish *que*) and a clause with a finite verb; but even so the "accusative and infinitive" is still found in some special cases, such as in French *je le vois venir*, "I can see him coming"; Spanish *le veo venir*, indeed, is still the usual way of expressing this meaning. It is anyhow important to realize that the replacement of the great majority of infinitive clauses by subordinate clauses introduced by a conjunction led to a strong extension of conjunctional subordination in general, these completive *that*-clauses being in themselves the most frequently used subordinate clauses. We have sometimes been told that Vulgar Latin used subordinate clauses less than before, but this just is not true; subordination survives throughout as an available and lively possibility. It is true, on the other hand, that the repertoire of subordinating conjunctions became slightly reduced over time.

There are two tendencies to note in the repertoire of conjunctions. The first is that some conjunctions expanded their functions. This is most obvious, indeed, with *quod*, which came to be a kind of "universal" conjunction; in the Classical language, *quod* had mainly been used as a causal and explanatory connective ("because"), apart from a few special cases, but in Late Latin, particularly in Late Vulgar Latin, *quod* turns up with other functions, including some that had previously been reserved for *cum* and *si*. Thus we find a *quod* of purpose ("in order that") in Saint Benedict of Nursia's *Regula Monachorum* (4): *non uelle dici sanctum antequam sit, sed prius esse, quod verius dicatur,* which means "not to want to be called a saint before you become one, but to be one first, in order to be called a saint more truthfully"; we find a *quod* with consecutive meaning ("so . . . that") in Palladius's *De ueterinaria medicina* (31.4): *uulnus ita insanabile facit, quod totus pes amputandus sit,* "it makes the wound so incurable that the whole leg has to be amputated"; we find a *quod* with comparative meaning ("as") in Tertullian's *De anima* (10): *incedunt . . . sine pedibus . . . quod angues,* "they come forward . . . without any feet . . . as snakes do"; we find a *quod* with temporal meaning ("when") in the *Formulae Andecauenses,* of the second half of the sixth century, (1a): *Annum quarto regnum domni nostri Childeberto reges, quod fecit minsus ille, dies tantus,* "in the fourth year of the reign of our lord King Childebert, when it was such and such a month, and such and such a day."

Another conjunction that expanded its meaning was *quomodo*; its function in Classical times was to mean "how," but in Vulgar Latin it can also be found with temporal meaning, "when," as in Antoninus of Placentia's *Itinerarium* (46): *uidi beatam Euphemiam per uisionem et beatum Antonium; quomodo uenerunt, sanauerunt me,* "in a vision I saw Saint Euphemia and Saint Anthony; when they came, they cured me." It could also be used causally, to mean "because."

The conjunctions *ut* and *cum* are found in even the most "vulgar" of texts, if not always very frequently, which suggests that they had not yet disappeared; but the extension of the uses of *quod* and *quomodo* was largely into functions previously expressed by *ut* and *cum,* which indirectly shows that the latter two were losing ground. This was to lead to the situation in Romance, where neither *ut* nor *cum* (as a conjunction) has left any trace (although it has been suggested that a descendant of *ut* might still exist in a southern Italian dialect), while a conjunction deriving from *quomodo* survives in every Romance area: thus Spanish and Portuguese *como,* Catalan *com,* Italian *come,* French *comme,* Rumanian *cum,* etc. And every Modern Romance language has a multipurpose conjunction (subordinating, causal, of purpose, etc.), which may or may not derive directly from the form *quod* but has certainly inherited the Vulgar functions of this word: thus Portuguese, Spanish, Catalan, and French *que,* Italian *che,* Rumanian *ca,* etc.

The second main tendency in the evolution of the repertoire of conjunctions concerns the creation and the increasingly general use of compound conjunctions combining a pronoun, sometimes preceded by a preposition, and a conjunction, usually *quod*. An exhaustive list of such cases cannot be given here, but one good example is *pro eo quod*, literally "for that which"; this combination was used occasionally in Classical times, but it only became frequent and unmarked, with a specifically causal meaning of "because," in the later period: thus Faustus of Riez (who died in 490), in his *Sermones* (25), wrote: *cum . . . animi dolore manducet pro eo quod aliis ieiunantibus et ipse non potest*, "that . . . he should eat with pain in his heart because he is unable to fast while others are doing so." Other more or less fixed and cohesive combinations are also found, including *ab eo quod, ex eo quod, in eo quod*, and *per id quod*, which often mean "because" too. These usages seem to have arisen once *quod* and *quia* came to be used commonly as simple subordinating conjunctions after verbs such as *dico* (I say) and *scio* (I know); that is, once *quod* was taking on several extra functions and was thus running the risk of ambiguity, speakers were trying to find alternatives that would be specifically understood to mean "because." Late Latin texts also show non-Classical combinations of adverb and conjunction such as *mox quod* (literally "soon that") to mean "as soon as" and *interim quod* (literally "meanwhile that") to mean "while." After the end of the Empire, particularly in the most obviously Vulgar texts, we see combinations of preposition and conjunction such as *post quod* (after that), *ante* or *antea quod* (before that); thus the *Lex Alamannorum*, of roughly A.D. 700 (version A), Law 50.1, has *si antea mortua fuerit, antea quod ille maritus eam quaesierit*, meaning "if she has died before her husband has gone to look for her." Romance has used a number of such compound conjunctions from the earliest times, and these probably derive from similar usages in Late Latin: for example, Old French *por co que*, Old Italian *per ciò che*, Modern Italian *perchè*, and Spanish *porque*, mean "because," and Old French *puis que* and Italian *poi chè* mean "after."

While on the subject of subordinate clauses, we should also mention indirect questions, and in particular the increasing use of *si* (originally "if") as an interrogative conjunction to mean "whether." *Si* had occasionally been used previously with an interrogative function, but this only became normal and frequent in Late Latin. Thus, for example, the *Vetus Latina*'s version of *Genesis* (37.32) was *cognosce si tunica filii tui est aut non*, "see now whether it is your son's robe or not," but Saint Jerome avoided this use of *si* in his own version, and the Vulgate has *utrum . . . an*, which are the Classical words for "whether . . . or." In this case, once again, the influence of Greek syntax may be seen here; in this sentence, and in others translated from Greek, the Latin *si* is used to render Greek εἰ, which meant both "if" and "whether." This would not imply that this use of *si* is merely a Grecism, though, since right from the earliest texts *si*, although predominantly hypothetical ("if"), could be used in an interrogative way: thus Plautus's *Miles gloriosus* (1256) reads *odore nasum sentiat, si intus sit*, "my nose will know from the smell if he is inside"; this shows that the possibility of such an extension of *si* was already inherent in Latin. This indirect interrogative use of *si* continued, and came to be normal in Romance.

The word *quare* was originally interrogative ("why?"), but it came to acquire a causal meaning ("because"), perhaps because of its regular use introducing indirect questions, as in, for example, Victor Vitensis (III.20): *quare contra praeceptum euangelii iurare uoluistis, iussit rex ut ciuitates . . . uestras numquam uideatis*, "because you wanted to swear against the precepts of the Gospels, the king has ordered that . . . you should never again see your home towns." Some Romance languages still have a causal conjunction that derives from *quare* as used in this way, particularly French (*car*) and Occitan.

Finally, in this section on subordinate clauses, we should note some of the developments in the so-called sequence of tenses. This is the name traditionally given to the fairly strict rule that existed in Classical Latin concerning the tenses to be used in subordinate clauses; this rule required a clear idea of the nature of tenses and the precise use of quite a subtle grammatical device, so it is perhaps only to be expected that the rule is relaxed in the Vulgar texts. One common and typical development, which was to continue in Romance, was this: in the Classical language, if a main verb in the past tense governed a subordinate clause containing a verb in the subjunctive mood whose reference was intended to be simultaneous with or later in time than that of the main verb, then the imperfect subjunctive was used; for example, *scripsi quid sentirem*, "I wrote what my feelings were." In such clauses, the pluperfect subjunctive was used when referring to an earlier time, as in *scripsi quid audiuissem*, "I wrote what it was that I had heard." But in the later texts, the pluperfect subjunctive was increasingly used instead of the imperfect subjunctive to refer to the same time as that of the main verb, or even to a later time, which thus led to a diminution of its unambiguously pluperfect reference; this may well have happened because the endings in [isse] were both more distinctive phonetically and more clearly "past" in themselves. Thus we find, in Lucifer of Cagliari's *De non conueniendo cum haereticis* (5), *directa est obsecratio ad Deum, (ut) . . . fuissemus segregati*, "a prayer was directed to God that . . . we should be separated" (that is, "in the future"); similarly, in Gregory of Tours's *Historia Francorum* (VII.10), *cecidisse fertur, ita ut uix manibus circunstantium sustentari potuisset*, "it is said that he fell in such a way that he could hardly be held up by the hands of his companions" (some manuscripts read *sustentare* here, the originally active infinitive, rather than the passive *sustentari*). The pluperfect subjunctive could even at times be used instead of the perfect subjunctive, which had been traditionally used to express previous tense reference in a subordinate clause after a main verb in the present tense; for example, Gregory of Tours's *Historia Francorum* (I.4): *increpant nobis hic haeretici cur scriptura sancta Dominum dixissit iratum* (with *dixissit* for the correct form *dixisset*), "the heretics are asking us here why the Holy Scripture wrote that the Lord was enraged." We saw above that the form of the original pluperfect subjunctive has survived in Romance, as in French [*que je*] *chantasse*, Italian *cantassi*, *cantasse*, Spanish *cantase*, etc., from *cantauissem*, but without its original pluperfect reference; these examples show that there were functional as well as formal developments in Late Vulgar Latin, which together effectively condemned to death the imperfect and perfect subjunctives such as *cantarem* and *cantauerim*.

7

VOCABULARY

1. Invariant Words

Invariant words are those that have no inflections; they are considered to be grammatical elements to some extent, since, although they indirectly refer to extralinguistic entities, their main function is to express relationships between the different parts of the sentence. This is certainly true of prepositions and conjunctions; it is much less true of adverbs, even though some of them, such as the interrogatives, have an obvious grammatical purpose. Invariant words are thus part of both the grammar and the lexicon, so it is unsurprising to find that the way they evolved in Vulgar Latin is related to the developments that we have already seen in grammatical structure.

The most noticeable tendency in the Vulgar Latin evolution of these words is the partial replacement of old synthetic forms with periphrases, analytical constructions including an element that explicitly expresses the function of the older one-word form. In the case of prepositions, and to some extent adverbs, this tendency can often be seen in the creation of pleonastic, or apparently pleonastic, combinations of two synonymous elements. It is interesting to observe that many of these combinations have survived in Romance. An example that is not pleonastic, in that the different meanings of both elements combine in the meaning of the compound, is the combination of *ab* (from) and *ante* (in front of) as *abante*: thus the *Vetus Latina*, in Leviticus (10.4), has *tollite fratres uestros abante faciem sanctorum* (carry your brethren from before the sanctuary), in which *abante* is not a Classical usage but can still be understood as a combination of the Classical meanings of its constituent parts; very soon, however, *abante* came just to mean the same as *ante*, eventually leading to French *avant*, Italian *avanti*, etc. Grammarians condemn the compounds *deintus*, *deforis*, and *depost*, which combined *de*, "from," with an existing preposition or adverb, but this just proves that these forms were indeed spoken: and they survive as, for example, French *dans* ("in," from *deintus*) and Occitan *defors* ("outside," from *deforis*). These combinations originally had a more precise function than simple *intus* or *foris*, corresponding to a desire for greater clarity concerning spatial relationships (although this may not always have been achieved): we find, for example, in *Epistula* 21.39 of Saint Jerome, *deintus quosdam . . . expellit foras* (expels some of them from inside to outside), where *deintus* does indeed signify "from inside" (since not all manuscripts of the Epistles contain this phrase, many editors have left it out of Jerome's text, considering it a later, "vulgar," addition). Some formations can only have been pleonastic from the start, however, including the compound use of *de ex* (literally "from from") as used in CIL XIV 5210, for example, *uixit cum eo de ex die uirginitatis suae*, "she lived with him ever since the day she lost her virginity." The French preposition *dès*, "since," goes back to this "vulgar" pairing, as does the *des-* of Spanish *después* ("after," from *de ex post*); similarly, the Italian *da* (from) goes back to *de ab*, a combination that is also attested in Vulgar texts.

Another way of forming more precise words than the old synthetic terms was by periphrasis, a procedure that was particularly used in the creation of new adverbs (to begin with, mainly temporal adverbs). These periphrases, which often replaced the former synthetic words, are of varying complexity, but they usually contained a nominal element. Thus *nunc* (now) was increasingly avoided in favor of *ad horam*, *hac hora* (at this time), *ad praesens*, or *in praesenti* (at present); Anthimus, for example, in his *De observatione ciborum* (14), wrote *de laredo uero . . . qualiter melius comedatur, ad hora expono*, "I will now explain about the best way to eat lard." Similarly, *tunc* (then) was often discarded in favor of *ea hora* or *illa hora* (at that time), and *diu* (for a long time) in favor of *longo tempore*, *multo tempore*, etc. Many of these periphrases survived into Romance, while the original word was often lost; several Romance words derive from expressions including *hora*, such as Old Spanish *agora* ("now," from *hac hora*; Modern *ahora*), and the Old or Modern French *or*, *ore*, *ores* (now), *lors*, *lores*, *alors* (then), and *encore* (still).

We have already seen examples of how the system of conjunctions developed in Vulgar Latin, most especially the subordinating conjunctions, in the preceding chapter; there, too, the creation of analytic expressions was the main method used.

2. Inflected Words

a) Lexical Substitutions

It would be impossible to describe here the complete evolution of the vocabulary, so I will confine myself to pointing out the main lines of development.

The original resources of the Latin vocabulary are partially renewed in Vulgar Latin. Quite a large number of the words that were perfectly normal in the Classical period come to be gradually replaced by alternatives; these alternatives are not new words in themselves, being no less part of the Latin vocabulary than the ones they replace, but are either new combinations of ancient elements or words that had hitherto had only a peripheral place in the lexical system. This is an important process, and the Vulgar texts are able to attest it directly; they often show a clear preference for such "new" vocabulary, avoiding the older alternative, which probably by then appeared to be suited to a more literary register only. The vocabulary that survives in Romance can in turn offer us a kind of control mechanism that is largely reliable as well as convenient.

Usually we can see the point of these changes, the reasons why speakers, usually unconsciously, preferred one word or expression to another. These reasons can naturally interact with each other at times; although they are classified separately below, this is just for the sake of clarity.

(A) It is often observable that words belonging to special inflectional paradigms or having complicated irregularities in their forms give way to simpler alternatives with commoner and more regular inflectional patterns. Substitutions of this kind are largely confined to verbs. Examples include the words for "eat": the original word for "I eat" was *edo*, with the infinitive either *edere* or *esse* (with long [eː], [eːsse]); this is the normal word in Plautus, much commoner than the prefixed form *comedere*. But in the later Vulgar texts, the word for "to eat" is much more commonly either *comedere* or *manducare* (indirectly derived from *mandere*, "chew"). In Saint Jerome's Vulgate, for example, both these verbs are common, while *esse* occurs, but only rarely. Romance vocabulary reflects this exactly; *edere/esse* does not survive at all, and Romance words derive either from *comedere* (such as Portuguese and Spanish *comer*) or from *manducare* (such as Catalan *menjar*, French *manger*, Italian *mangiare*, and Rumanian *mînca*). The point behind this substitution is fairly clear; *edere/esse* had highly irregular inflections, some of which were the same as forms of *esse*, "to be" (with originally short [e], [esse]), once the opposition between long and short vowels ceased to be distinctive, which must have been inconvenient; the substitute verbs had regular inflections and a longer and more distinctive phonetic individuality.

The same reasons could be adduced to explain the common replacement of the irregular verb *ferre* (to bring) with the largely synonymous *portare*, of the deponent *loqui* (to speak) with *parabolare* and *fabulare*, and the partial disappearance of *ire* (to go), some of whose forms survive (e.g., in Spanish *ir*), but the majority of which have been replaced by forms of either *ambulare* or *vadere*. In the cases mentioned so far, these processes of replacement seem to have reached their peak in the period immediately preceding the emergence in writing of Romance; but other such cases were only just beginning in Vulgar Latin and came to complete fruition later in Romance. This applies, for example, to the verb *iacere* (lie down); *conlocare* or *collocare* (originally "to put," "to place") is used reflexively with this meaning in some of the Vulgar texts; thus the sixth-century writer Jordanes, in his *De summa temporum uel origine actibusque gentis Romanorum* (254), wrote *Cleopatra . . . iuxta suum se conlocauit Antonium*, "Cleopatra laid herself down next to her lover Anthony." Both words remained available and in competition in

France; Old French *gésir*, from *iacere*, is common still, and it is only later that *coucher*, from *collocare*, became the normal word for this meaning; *giacere* survives as the normal word in Italy; in Spanish, on the other hand, *yacer* usually refers to the dead (here lies), *colgar* (from *collocare*) means "hang," and "to lie" is *acostar* (formed off *costa*, "side").

Another way of achieving greater simplicity is by reforming the verb root; thus the deponent verb *obliviscor* (I forget) was restructured into a regular verb based on the participle *oblitus*, and a reconstructable but unattested infinitive [oblitáre] underlies French *oublier* and Spanish *olvidar*.

(B) It was easy to replace some short words with longer ones of greater phonetic substance. The preference in this case was motivated by communicative needs; as phonetic changes progressed, the shortest words could risk losing their phonetic individuality by becoming indistinguishable from other words or at least very similar to them, and this in turn could lead to misunderstandings and uncertainties on the part of the listener. This explains why the word *bucca*, originally meaning "cheek" and mostly used only in colloquial registers, often came to be preferred to the original word for "mouth," *os* (with a long [o:]), which had the genitive *oris*. This *os* was an insubstantial word anyway, and once the distinctiveness of vowel length disappeared, it was inconveniently similar in many forms to *os*, genitive *ossis*, "bone," originally with short [o]. *Os*, "mouth," survives nowhere in Romance, and most of Romance now has derivatives of *bucca* as the ordinary word for mouth (Portuguese, Spanish, and Catalan *boca*, French *bouche*, Italian *bocca*). Some verbs also come into this category; the Classical word for "weep" was *flere*, but in Late and Vulgar texts, at least, it gives way to *plorare*; the Romance words all come from *plorare* (French *pleurer*, Spanish *llorar*, etc.) or *plangere* (e.g., Italian *piangere*).

But in the majority of cases the word that replaces the insubstantial Classical one is merely an affixed form of it. The most notable case concerns the "vulgar" liking for diminutives. Diminutives must have been not only widely used but thought of as a colloquial feature. The anonymous author of the *Appendix Probi* includes many diminutive forms among those he disapproves of; for example, he mentions a form *oricla*, which is a variant spelling of *auricula*, the diminutive of *auris*, "ear," and this is the word from which the whole of Romance has derived its word for "ear": Rumanian *ureche*, Italian *orecchio*, French *oreille*, Catalan *orella*, Spanish *oreja*, Portuguese *orelha* all mean "ear" rather than "little ear" (although the *Appendix Probi* also mentions several forms that have not survived in Romance, such as *iuuenculus* and *iuuenclus*, diminutives of *iuuencus*, "bullock"; *anucula* and *anucla*, diminutives of *anus*, "old woman"). Similarly, many Romance words for "knee" come from the diminutive form *genuculum*, which replaces *genu*: Italian *ginocchio*, French *genou*, Old Spanish *hinojo*, etc. There are also cases in which both the original and the diminutive survive, such as *agnellus* and *agnus*, "lamb," in Italian *agnello* and *agno*, French *agneau*; the word for "sun" comes from *solem* in Rumanian *soare*, Italian *sole*, and Spanish *sol*, but from a diminutive in *-iculum* in French *soleil* and Occitan *solelh*. This last example helps illuminate the reasons why diminutives were used at all in such cases, when they do not mean "little": the diminutive form only replaced the original [sole] in places where word-final vowels other than [a] were eventually dropped, since this development led to ambiguity between the words written *solem* and *solum* (only); using the diminutive form instead thus corresponds to a simple need for formal clarity, having nothing to do with its meaning or with any supposed popular psychological misconceptions about the nature of the sun.

These affixed forms with greater phonetic substance, which are for that reason preferred to the root word alone, are more often formed with these diminutives than with any other kind of affix. This may in part be due to some emotional cause, but can be explained simply enough by internal structural factors alone. The difference in meaning between the simple root noun and its diminutive form is smaller and less important than the difference between the meaning of the root and that of any other affixed form—that is, an *agnellus* is still an *agnus*—and this factor is in itself enough to explain why a form strengthened with a diminutive affix should be the most readily available substitute for a noun felt to be of insufficient phonetic substance.

It is worth pointing out that some cases fall into both the above categories, both into category A, in which an irregular verb is replaced by a regularly inflected one, and into category B, in which a short word is replaced by a longer one. Thus *esse* (eat) is not only a morphologically less regular verb than *manducare*, for example, but also a shorter one, more liable to suffer confusion with homonymic words; the same applies to *ire* as compared with *ambulare*, and several other cases. There is a historical reason for this; the most archaic verbs are often both the least morphologically regular verbs and the shortest, being built in their majority on an unsuffixed monosyllabic stem.

(C) Sometimes there is no visible formal reason for a word to be replaced by a synonym, but a semantic reason can be envisaged instead. A word can have some nuance of meaning that makes it more suited to the lives and attitudes of the people of the time, and thus comes to be used in preference to a more semantically neutral ancient word, even though they both have more or less the same meaning. Thus the word *caballus*, originally "workhorse" or "gelding," was used in Vulgar Latin and is still used in all Romance (French *cheval*, Italian *cavallo*, Rumanian *cal*, Catalan *cavall*, Spanish *caballo*, Portuguese *cavalo*), replacing the Classical word for "horse," *equus*, which lacked these everyday connotations (although *equa* survived in the feminine, as in Spanish *yegua*). Similarly, *battalia* or *battualia*, which originally referred to "battle exercises carried out by soldiers or gladiators," everyday events in military camps, came to be used in all areas in preference to the older, more solemn, and less practical word *proelium*; thus we have Italian *battaglia*, French *bataille*, Rumanian *bătaie*, Catalan and Spanish *batalla*, Portuguese *batalha*. The word *hostis*, "enemy," acquires the meaning of "army" (enemy or not) in about the sixth century, completely replacing the previous word for "army," *exercitus*; this is just a lexical consequence of the dread that all people feel of all armies.

Sometimes the semantic reasons are less straightforward, and the change could be better described as stylistic. The exact nature of such a development is not always easy for us to reconstruct. The Latin word for "beautiful" was *pulcher*, which survives nowhere in Romance; perhaps it was felt to be a needlessly solemn and abstract word. In any event, more down to earth synonyms such as *bellus* and *formosus* were preferred instead. Similarly, the word for "small," *paruus*, was replaced everywhere by words that seem really to come from the nursery, such as *pitinnus*, *pisinnus*, *putillus* (teeny). The metaphorical use of *testa*, "cooking pot," for "skull," and then simply "head," as in French *tête* (or "forehead," as in Portuguese *testa*), may have begun as a kind of joke; but there are formal factors involved here too, since the original word for "head" was the neuter noun *caput*, and although this word survives in most Romance areas (e.g., French *chef*, Italian *capo*), it had that improbable final [-t] and an inflectional system that would have seemed most unusual in the context of the simplified Vulgar Latin systems, so we can understand why the word *testa* would often have been deliberately preferred for its simpler morphology. Its metaphorical nature need not have lasted long; it soon became another literal alternative for "head."

b) Semantic Changes

No general formula can sum up the semantic developments in Vulgar Latin. At first sight, it may seem as though there is a general tendency to move from abstract to concrete meanings, for it is true that many words originally used to refer to abstractions, psychological phenomena, etc., came to be used increasingly to refer to some tangible manifestation of the abstraction concerned. On many tombstones, for example, the inscription uses the word *memoria* (originally "memory") to refer to the tombstone itself. Similarly, in several late documents, the word *testimonium* (originally "testimony") is used to refer to the actual witnesses; thus in the eighth-century *Formulae Senonenses recentiores* (3), *ipse abba uel suus auocatus . . . taliter dixerunt quod testimonia homines Francos presentare potebant* means "the abbot himself, or his lawyer . . . declared that they were able to put forward some men from the Franks as witnesses." The same happens with the word *solacium* (originally "solace"), which is often used to refer simply to material help, as in Gregory of Tours's *Historia Francorum* (II.32): *si mihi ad persequendum fratrem meum praebueris solatium, ut eum bello interficere . . . possim*, meaning "if you give me your help against my brother, so that I can kill him in battle." This also happens with the adjective *recens* (recent), less common and more exact than its partial synonym *nouus* (new), which came to be used with the meaning of "fresh" or even "cold" (since, for example, freshly gathered water tends to be cold); thus Apicius, in his *De re coquinaria* (chapter 125) refers to *aquam recentem*, meaning "fresh water." In Rumania, the word survives with that meaning: *rece* means "fresh." Similarly, the word *pacare* originally meant "placate," "pacify," but over most of the Romance area it survives with the meaning of "pay" (in French *payer*, Spanish *pagar*, Italian *pagare*, etc.); here the psychological action of pacifying has been developed into the concrete meaning of satisfying somebody's demands through the giving of money. In this way a number of fairly unexpected changes can be illuminated to some extent; words used to refer to complex intangible realities tend to develop in this direction, coming to be used to refer to simpler and more everyday experience.

But there are also changes that seem, from a logical point of view, to be exactly the opposite of what we have just been describing, that is, which change from concrete to abstract, or from particular to general. Even so, these generalizations of meaning seem psychologically to be evidence of exactly the same uncertainty in the manipulation of difficult or complex abstractions as we saw in the changes that traveled in the other direction. When someone needed to refer to an abstraction or an action that lacked a material manifestation, it was easy to use terms whose usual meaning made the idea more comprehensible in tangible terms. Many Christian funeral inscriptions in northwestern Gaul, for example, use the word *patres*, literally "fathers," to mean "parents" (more usually expressed by *parentes*). Similarly, Late Latin often renders the abstract notion of "remain" with the verb *sedere* (sit); thus Egeria's *Itinerarium* (5.1) contains *illa ualle . . . ubi sederant filii Israhel dum Moyses ascenderet in montem Dei*, meaning "that valley . . . where the sons of Israel stayed while Moses went up the Lord's mountain" (and several forms of *sedere* join the paradigms of "to be" in Romance). Another such case, among many, is that of *focus* (hearth), which replaces *ignis* as the word used to refer to "fire."

One group of semantic changes is worth considering separately; instead of being explicable through logical or psychological considerations, this group can be illuminated by historical and ideological circumstances. The early Christians gave a number of existing Latin words a particular nuance of their own, as they adapted them to the requirements of their religion. One example of this is the Latin word *caro*, "meat," and its derived adjective *carnalis*, which were used as pejorative terms by early Christian writers referring to what they saw as sins of the flesh (that is, sexual desires). This meaning came to take over that of the adjective in particular; thus, for example, Modern Spanish *carne* just means "meat," but *carnal* means "sexual." It was the Christian texts that gave the word *gentes* (people) a specific meaning of "gentiles" (or "pagans"), the word *beatus* (happy) a more specific meaning of "saintly," and the phrase *dies iudicii* the precise reference to "(the final) day of judgment" rather than any other day of any other judgment. This is also the context in which such words as *salus* (health), *spiritus* (spirit), *fides* (faith), *credere* (believe), and many others acquired a specialized religious sense that their Romance derivatives still tend to imply now— thus French *salut*, *esprit*, *foi*, *croire* (specifically implying a Christian belief in God), Spanish *salud* (of the soul), *espíritu*, *fe*, *creer* (in God), and so on.

c) Affixation and Compounding

Vulgar Latin was not particularly innovative as regards its techniques of creating new words via affixation and compounding. It acquired a number of neologisms, or apparent neologisms, that did not exist in the Classical language and freely used several prefixes and suffixes, but these are not themselves new. We have already mentioned the remarkable productivity of diminutive suffixes in Vulgar Latin; several others were also often used to create a new word. One example is *-arius* (feminine *-aria*, neuter *-arium*), available to create nouns and adjectives; the inscriptions have preserved for us a number of new nouns with this suffix that refer to particular professions. Thus a *saccarius* was a sack maker, a *burgarius* was a soldier who served in a *burgus* (castle, fort), a *pecuarius* looked after a herd of cows (*pecus*), and the word *centenarius* could be used in preference to the normal *centurio* for "centurion." The suffix *-arium* (usually here preferred to *-arius*) could be used to create words referring to utensils and containers, such as *atramentarium* (inkwell), *panarium* (breadbasket), and *pultarius* (porridge plate). These forms need not all have been Late or Vulgar, in fact; they are mostly precise words that could easily have been in existence in Classical times and used in speech even by the most educated groups in society where relevant, without, even so, being found in literary texts.

Verbal suffixes available included *-icare*, an ancient suffix with an originally frequentative sense ("to do something repeatedly"), which was used to create many Vulgar words; *carricare*, for example, survives in most Romance languages, such as Spanish, *cargar*, and French, *charger* (load); Romance words such as French *bouger* (stir) and Italian *bulicare* (bubble) suggest that there existed in Late Latin an unattested form *bullicare as a frequentative of *bullire* (boil).

Most of the suffixes used in Vulgar Latin are not themselves new, although it is worth pointing out that one of the most widely used was Greek in origin; the verb-creating suffix *-izare* (or *-idiare*) comes from the Greek suffix -ίζειν and was particularly in favor among the Christians, who formed such words as *baptizare* and *scandalizare*.

Vulgar Latin created a large number of compounds (words formed by combining two other whole words). These are based, not always felicitously, on traditional patterns. Some of the words disapproved of in the *Appendix Probi* are unusually "barbarous" in appearance and have not survived in that form—*aquiductus*, for example ("aqueduct," as opposed to the more correct *aquae ductus*), and *terrimotium* ("earthquake," as opposed to *terrae motus*). One kind of compound was going to have a particularly happy future in Romance; the combination of an adjective in the ablative with the noun *mente* (mind, spirit, disposition) could be used with adverbial force. Thus, for example, *caeca mente*, literally "with a blind mind," could be used to mean "blindly" (as still in, e.g., Spanish *ciegamente*). Originally, the independent meaning of *mente* was still there in the compound, as had been the case, for example, in Virgil's *Aeneid* (IV.105): *sensit enim simulata mente locutam*, meaning "realized that she had spoken with a feigned mind" (that is, she had not expressed her real feelings); but the construction gradually became rigidified, until in the end *mente* came to be no more than the adverb-forming suffix *-mente*, still productive for this purpose in French *-ment*, Spanish and Italian *-mente*, etc.

d) Foreign Words

Vulgar Latin contained far more words borrowed from other languages than literary texts did. This is understandable; technicians, craftsmen, professionals practising any kind of practical trade, were often foreign themselves or at least of non-Latin descent—most notably Greek or Semitic—and, even more important, most technical knowledge (other than agricultural expertise) was itself imported, particularly from Greece. Under these circumstances we can see why a majority of technical terms are in fact Greek. A work on human or animal medicine was full of Greek terms, sometimes explicitly acknowledged as such, as in the *Mulomedicina Chironis* (469): *Si quod iumentum uitio subrenali prensum fuerit, quod appellatur graece nefrites*, "when a beast of burden is caught by a pain in the lower part of the kidneys, known in Greek as 'nephrites.'" But more often than not they were used unselfconsciously. The hundreds of such unacknowledged Greek borrowings in the *Mulomedicina Chironis* include *cataplasma* (a plaster), its verbal derivative *cataplasmare*, *paralisis*, and *aterapeutus* (unhealed). One of these Greek borrowings, originally a veterinary term only, *gamba* ("knee joint," from Greek καμπή, "turning point") came to replace the original word for "leg," *crus*, in most Romance languages: thus French *jambe*, Italian *gamba*, Logudorese Sardinian *kamba*, etc.

Cooking terms were often of Greek origin too. It is interesting to realize that the names of simple utensils and common dishes were Latin, whereas more complicated utensils and less common but more luxurious dishes had Greek names: thus *puls* (porridge) and *farcimen* (sausage meat) are native Latin words, while *isicium* (a kind of rissole), *embamma* (a kind of strong sauce or acidic condiment), and others are taken from Greek. One Latin term that was calqued on the Greek was *ficatum* (*iecur*), "(goose's liver) fattened with figs," modeled on the Greek συκωτὸν ἧπαρ, and the participle *ficatum* became the origin of all the words for "liver" in Romance, such as Spanish *hígado*, French *foie*, Italian *fegato*, and Rumanian *ficat*. Similarly, although religion is not exactly a technical field, Christianity brought in an important group of specialized Greek terms, including *euangelium*, *angelus*, *propheta*, *episcopus* (bishop), *presbyter* (priest), *martyr*, and many others.

Before the end of the Empire, the contributions made to the Latin vocabulary by languages other than Greek were small in comparison. Some Celtic words were taken in, such as *braca* (pants), *carrum* (wagon), and *camisia* (shirt); and a few rare Germanic words, including *ganta* ("wild duck" or "wild goose," which survived in, e.g., Old French *jante* and Occitan *ganta*) and *brutis* (daughter-in-law), were used here and there in inscriptions. Presumably the number of Celtic words that were used in spoken Latin during the period of Gaulish-Latin bilingualism must have been quite high, and indeed a good many words of Celtic origin survive to this day in French and Occitan; but very few of these borrowings are visible in the Vulgar Latin texts. After the end of the Empire several areas were occupied by Germanic-speakers, and as a result more Germanic words were borrowed into Latin in those areas at that time; but this topic lies outside our present framework of investigation.

8

MORE GENERAL PROBLEMS

1. The End of the History of Latin

In one sense, the history of Latin is continuing even now. Latin was used through the Middle Ages and the first part of the modern period, in most of Europe, as the language of intellectual life and of many official spheres of activity; and it was the language used by the Catholic Church until very recently, in its liturgy and institutions. Because of the basic role it has played in European civilization, Latin is still widely taught and studied in many secondary schools in Europe and America, as well as in all the important universities. (It is also quite commonly said that Latin is still alive in its guise as the Romance languages and that in this way its history has been continuous; but this ignores rather too conveniently the essential structural differences that exist between Latin and Romance.) We need to bear in mind a fundamental point here; a language is a means of communication that is learned naturally and spontaneously, used from childhood by every member of a speech community in every aspect of life. So its history comes to an end—or, to put it another way, the language becomes a "dead" language—when it stops functioning in this way and is no longer anybody's natural mother tongue. This applies to Latin too, and as a result it is necessary and important for us to ask at what time, and through what evolutionary stages, Latin changed from being the living natural mother tongue, in those places where it was spoken, to being a language foreign to all, which could not be used or understood even by Romance-speakers except as the result of deliberate and systematic study.

In 1931 the French historian Ferdinand Lot asked this question, in a famous and most helpful article entitled "A quelle époque a-t-on cessé de parler latin?" The title of the article was not well phrased, however, since with the help of specialist study it has always been possible to speak Latin for particular purposes and in particular circumstances, even though Latin has been a "dead" language for a long time. But it is worth taking seriously the train of thought that Lot started here, since the answer that he came up with proved to be the first stage in elaborating a more acceptable response. When Lot used the word "Latin," he had in mind the standardized Classical Latin as used by the best authors in the Classical tradition, and as a result he came to the conclusion that Latin had come to the end of its history as soon as the way in which people spoke began to differ from the way in which they wrote. If we start from this assumption, then all we have to do is work out a rough date for the appearance of a clear difference between traditional written usage and spoken, "vulgar," usage in some part of the linguistic structure, and on the basis of this date we would be able to decide when Latin had "died." We could well come to the conclusion, for example, that the system of spoken vowels was different from that represented in the written mode of the language by the fourth century; that some of the changes in the consonant system, such as the loss of [-m] and the assibilation of [t] and [k] before [j] (to [ts]), had been completed by the fifth century at the latest; and that the traditional declension system was being replaced by a system with just two or three cases (depending on the region) at that same time; so perhaps from this we should conclude that the language spoken at the end of the Roman Empire was no longer Latin. But if it was not Latin, then what language was it? It was certainly not Romance, since many of the essential and characteristic constituent parts of Romance were not in existence at all at that time, such as the preponderant or exclusive use of prepositional phrases for syntactic functions other than the subject or the direct object, or the existence of a new periphrastic system of verb paradigms alongside the older ones.

It seems, as a result, that an answer to this question based merely on a separation between written and spoken usages is not a sufficient answer in itself. Differences, to a greater or lesser degree, between the traditional written form of a language and the spoken form are very common; they become almost inevitable, in fact, as a language develops, and the existence of such differences does not imply that the language has died and stopped being the same language it was. Contemporary English and French are sufficiently convincing examples in this respect. In both English and French there are remarkable differences between the written form of many words and any phonological transcription of the same words, differences that are often unpredictable and unsystematic. The divergence between written and spoken French even includes details of the grammar: for example, the majority of noun plural forms are distinguished from the singular in the written mode alone, and the written form distinguishes between several personal inflections of verbs that sound the same in speech. Even so, we can hardly doubt that French is a single language, essentially one language rather than two, and entirely a living language still despite the remarkable differences that there certainly are between its written and spoken modes.

At this point we should bear in mind that nobody at all in the fifth century, or even in the sixth, to judge by the admittedly small amount of evidence we have, doubted that the spoken language used in the Romanized areas was Latin or that the written form of that language, however traditional and "correct," and the spoken form, however uneducated the speaker, were different aspects of the same single language, belonging to the same speech community. For an example, we can consider Saint Caesarius of Arles, writing in the first half of the sixth century. In one of his *Sermones* (6.3) he laments that the country people in his diocese knew by heart and sang love songs, which he describes as being *diabolica et . . . turpia* (devilish and . . . immoral), while they would be able to learn and recite or sing the Creed, the Lord's Prayer, and even hymns more easily and with less effort (*celerius et melius*). The linguistic implication of what he says is unambiguous: for Caesarius, who knew very well what the life of his parishioners was like, the language of these love songs, undoubtedly part of popular culture, and the language of the biblical texts, which were undoubtedly Latin despite the occasional "vulgar" feature, were parts of the same language; the people's choice of register was not made according to linguistic competence but was the result of a moral or even religious attitude. And when the sacred texts were read aloud, undoubtedly their pronunciation was different from that of earlier centuries; but the readers and listeners would never have been in a position to realize that this was so, with the result that the sacred texts, orally presented and perceived, and the normal ordinary speech patterns of uneducated people, were not too different; both could fit inside the one essential linguistic concept, Latin. And similar evidence from all over the Romance area leads us to similar conclusions concerning the period up to the middle of the seventh century; the written language, however many "vulgar" features it did or did not contain, and the spoken language were always drifting gradually further apart, naturally, but in the linguistic consciousness of the speakers of the time it was still one language, and that one language was still thought of as Latin. Thus the fact that the spoken language and the written language were not identical is not in itself sufficient evidence from which to conclude that Latin was no longer a living language.

It might be possible instead to decide on a rough date for the death of Latin on purely structural grounds; we could undertake an analysis of the probable timing of the linguistic transformations that the language went through, and fix the turning point between Latin and Romance in this way. Unfortunately, if we use this kind of method we will very soon realize that no clear chronological boundary of this sort can be drawn between Latin and Romance, since the relevant changes in linguistic structure do not coincide with each other. Indeed, they continue over a period of many centuries. The basic transformation in the vowel system, the loss of phonological length, happened, as we have seen, over the last two centuries of the Empire itself, but the main transformations in the consonant system must have happened significantly later than that; the weakening of the intervocalic plosives was in general beginning to occur only at the end of the Empire, and, where it happened, the loss of [-t] and [-s] in word-final position was later still. As regards morphology, there was the same kind of unevenness in the rate of change of different inflectional systems. The declension system was beginning to collapse already by the end of the Empire, although its eventual disappearance was not complete until the second half of the first millennium; the verb system, however, seems to have remained virtually intact throughout the fifth century, since, although some of the periphrastic expressions had come into general use by then, such as the auxiliary use of *habeo* with the infinitive or with the past participle, these expressions were still a long way short of becoming grammaticalized as regular verb paradigms with a fixed structure and meaning; and the specifically Romance features of the verb inflection system were not going to come into general usage until much later. That is, the transformation of the language, from structures we call Latin into structures we call Romance, lasted from the third or fourth century until the eighth. Any more precise chronological cut between Latin and Romance would be quite arbitrary from this point of view, based on the changes in linguistic structure alone. The most that we could do to narrow the period down would be to say that the structure of the language spoken as the Empire came to its end was still essentially that which had been inherited from earlier Latin, although different in some respects from the spoken language we can reconstruct for Classical times, while, on the other hand, the language spoken in the later centuries of the first millennium A.D. was a language of rather a different kind. We have to conclude that basing our decision on criteria of a structural kind alone does not lead us to any more precise idea of how to decide when the spoken language stopped being Latin and started being Romance.[1]

If we want to come up with clear chronological limits with any validity, we will have to look to criteria beyond those of mere linguistic structure; since the communicative function is central to the use of a language, the nature of communication can help to illuminate the real consequences of the structural modifications within a language. Thus a more helpful criterion is that of the continuing *intelligibility* of

---

1. In the past some scholars came to a very early date for this divide on the basis of any novelty at all discovered in Latin, usually, in practice, phonetic; that is, these Romanists felt moved to claim that the language was already Romance on the basis of the discovery of a few symptoms of what would indeed later be identifying features of Romance. So some talked of Italian as existing in the first century or of French as existing in the third. Remarks like this ignored the structure of the language in general, the facts of Latin, and the actual history of oral communication at the time, and were hypotheses with no validity at all even as they were being written.

the language. From this perspective we can say that Latin became a dead language as soon as people without any literary education stopped being able to understand written Latin texts, either in its Classical form or in the more "vulgar" form that the language took in some of the works of post-Classical authors. And since throughout the second half of the first millennium A.D. most people were illiterate, the ability to understand the Latin language meant in practice the ability to understand texts when delivered orally, read aloud or recited. (We could add that many of those who had indeed learned to recognize the written letters only had sporadic contact with an actual written text, if that.) So the date we are trying to identify here is that at which the Romanized people of Europe could no longer understand texts that were read aloud or recited to them. And we do in fact have available some data concerning this. It seems certain that in the sixth century, and quite likely into the early part of the seventh century, people in the main Romanized areas could still largely understand the biblical and liturgical texts and the commentaries (of greater or lesser simplicity) that formed part of the rites and of religious practice, and that even later, throughout the seventh century, saints' lives written in Latin could be read aloud to the congregations with an expectation that they would be understood. The recent work of Michel Banniard and Marc van Uytfanghe is particularly illuminating in this respect (see the Bibliography). We can also deduce, however, that in Gaul, from the central part of the eighth century onward, many people, including several of the clerics, were not able to understand even the most straightforward religious texts, such as the Creed and the Lord's Prayer, for Charlemagne, king of the Franks from 768, felt on more than one occasion that he should remind his bishops that they had a duty to take steps to ensure that the congregation and the clergy could understand, for example, what it was that they were asking the Lord for when reciting the Lord's Prayer.

A few decades later, the regional church council held at Tours in 813 decreed that the sermons should be pronounced according to the *lingua romana rustica*, so that the listeners could understand them better. This famous decree makes explicit a situation that had been perceptible for several decades, as we have seen. We could conclude, then, that at least in Gaul the structural changes that the spoken language had undergone had led in the first half of the eighth century to a break in communication between the natural mother tongue, used by everybody, and the inherited Latin, used in texts. If we want a date, then, we could say that Latin "died" in the first part of the eighth century.[2]

There is no reason to suppose that the date for the conceptual separation of Latin and Romance was necessarily the same in every Romance-speaking area, not least since by this time the linguistic system was evolving in different ways and at different speeds in different places. In Italy, for example, the first signs we can see that people were consciously aware of a difference between their everyday language and the written practice of Latin texts date from the second half of the tenth century. On the Iberian Peninsula, the first signs of this development are found in the *Glosas Emilianenses* and *Silenses*, which used to be dated to the late tenth century but are now more commonly assigned to the second half of the eleventh century. These geographical differences for dating the "death" of Latin and the independent "birth" of Romance are due to factors that are still not clear; it is likely that the early and radical nature of some of the linguistic transformations that took place in the territory originally known as Gaul helped to make this development quicker there than elsewhere (such as the general loss of syllable-final vowels other than [a] in the Romance of the area, between the seventh and eighth centuries).

2. The Geographical Diversification of Latin

There are good reasons to believe that Latin during the time of the Empire already had geographical variations. These differences between

---

2. These problems have been clarified to a large extent by the work of the English Romance philologist Roger Wright (see the bibliography for details). Wright sees the decisive moment in the conceptual break between Latin and Romance as being the Carolingian "Renaissance" of the late eighth century, in particular the renewal of Latin, the process that the scholars of the time called *renovatio* and Wright calls the "invention of Medieval Latin," which even changed its pronunciation (advocating one sound for every letter). This would have created such a large gap between the normal Romance and the reformed Latin that it acted as the catalyst for the speakers to feel that they were indeed two separate languages (what Banniard calls the *prise de conscience* of the new situation). This assessment can only be

the regions where Latin was the natural first language of communication of the population were of various types. Later on, we can even talk of regional "dialects" of Latin.³ We can suppose this partly on the basis of generalities that have been discovered to be empirically true for the study of all languages; when a language is used over a wide and disparate geographical area, influenced by widely varying external factors of an ethnic and sociocultural type, geographical variants can arise that are noticeably different from each other despite the fact that they all form part of a single linguistic system. This is what has happened to Modern European languages such as English, Spanish, Portuguese, and French, which have been extended overseas by colonial enterprises and thus come to be spoken in different continents; but it also true that similar geographical divergence arises within languages that cover a much smaller area than these. As we saw in the Introduction, Latin was used as a native language or as a second language in the whole of the western Mediterranean basin, the whole of Italy, a large part of the Balkans, and much of central Europe, so it is hard to believe that it can have remained geographically homogeneous over the whole area for several centuries. Furthermore, some data can confirm these suspicions for us; there is a comment in the *Vita Severi* (in the *Historia Augusta*), concerning the emperor Severus, who was of African origin, to the effect that "he kept all his life a pronunciation that sounded rather African," *Afrum quiddam usque ad senectutem sonans*. There is also a famous comment of Saint Jerome's, made in his commentary on Saint Paul's Epistle to the Galatians (2.3), that Latin changes continuously "according to both place and time," *et regionibus . . . et tempore*. These are just general statements,

---

partly correct, however, since it seems clear that in Gaul the realization that there were problems in communication arose some decades before, rather than after, the first effective measures of linguistic reform. For the prehistory of Romance and the early history of Spanish, however, Wright's work has become essential.

3. This was probably true of the whole vast area ruled from Rome except those areas that almost exclusively used Greek. And there must also have been an earlier stage of Latin dialectalization within Italy, as Italic and other groups adopted the Latin of Rome and as Latin-speakers settled in the other parts of the peninsula. We do not know a great deal about this early stage, when the other languages of the peninsula, such as Oscan, Umbrian, and also Etruscan, were gradually disappearing, although some ancient authors, including Varro, give us isolated snatches of information.

of course, which tell us nothing about the nature of the differences themselves, and unfortunately there are almost no references made with greater detail, references that could thus be used for linguistic purposes (although a few are mentioned below). The main reason for assuming that there must have been some regional variation is the existence of the different Romance languages themselves, which could be seen as just the temporal continuations of regional variations within Latin.

And yet, despite these apparently excellent reasons for believing in regional divergences of this type, we cannot avoid admitting that during the whole Latin period we can only glimpse a tiny amount of divergence within the actual written data. In texts of all kinds, literary, technical, and all others, the written Latin of the first five or six centuries A.D. looks as if it were territorially homogeneous, even in its "vulgar" registers. It is only in later texts, of the seventh and eighth centuries, that we are able to see in the texts geographical differences that seem to be the precursors of similar differences in the subsequent Romance languages. Scholars have for some time been aware of differences between the late Merovingian documents of the early eighth century and those from Lombard Italy of the same period; for example, the Merovingian texts still keep a distinction between the nominative and the other case endings, thanks to the survival of final [-s] and -s, which is an early sign of what was later going to be attested in Old French and Occitan texts, while in the Italian documents the -s (and thus probably also the [-s]) is on its way out and the morphological distinction that depended on it is also rare. Different scholars have reacted to this general lack of territorial differentiation in the texts before the late seventh century in different ways; some have assumed from this that Late and Vulgar Latin was much the same everywhere until that date, leading to the hypothesis that the territorial differentiation did not occur until shortly before the emergence in texts of the separately written Romance dialects; others have taken the opposite view, putting forward the hypothesis that written texts were by their nature symptoms of traditional orthographical and linguistic prescriptions and thus cannot be used as evidence for the earliest history of Romance differentiation, and that the genuine processes of evolution would necessarily have implied an early dialectalization as well and can only be reconstructed by looking backward from the comparative evidence of the later attested Romance forms.

The last few decades have seen a more nuanced assessment of the situation than either of these approaches. We should note in the first place that some authors of the fourth century, and more in the fifth, including Saint Augustine, and some grammarians, such as Consentius, did mention specific details of local usage, in particular the way that Africans did not distinguish between short and long vowels (these were quoted in section 4.1 above). This is an important detailed reference that has made it possible to reconstruct the nature of the transformation of the vowel system, but it also shows that there were noticeable differences between the speech habits of different regions. At the same time, however, it shows that these differences still had a limited significance. If there had existed by this time serious practical problems concerning comprehension, these writers would surely have said so. In addition, the minutely detailed analysis of the imperial and the Christian inscriptions that has recently been carried out has made it possible to sketch an outline of this process that is certainly schematic but also seems to be authentic; the conclusion is that even though the "vulgar" features that are present in these inscriptions are (generally speaking) the same in every region, the statistical distribution of the innovatory features does indeed differ from region to region. This means that although similar changes happened in every place, they occurred at different rates. Naturally, in evaluating statistics, linguists have to avoid some pitfalls; differences in frequencies of "vulgar" features, as everyone realizes, may be due to differences in cultural levels between regions rather than to differences in language. But there are methods, easy to understand, that are widely used to counteract this possibility: proportions inside one region are usually specific (for example, one region has more confusions than would be proportionally foreseen in back vowels; another has a lower proportion of these but a higher one in some other respect), and a comparison of these specific features necessarily leads to linguistically relevant conclusions. So, for instance, during the time of the Empire itself, southern Italy and Africa were far more conservative as regards their vocalic system than Gaul and the North of Italy were, while, on the other hand, the consonant system in the southern regions was considerably more affected by developments than it was in, for example, Gaul; thus phenomena such as the confusion between the labials (see section 4.2c), the weakening of some of the word-final consonants, and some palatalizations are attested first at this time in Rome and the more southerly areas of the Empire and extend later to Greece. So it seems likely that in imperial times a slight amount of geographical variation did slowly arise in Latin, affecting pronunciation in particular but perhaps also a few morphological details (ignoring, of course, the wide differences we find in personal and place names, due to the different ethnic origins of the populations of different areas); this kind of divergence posed no threat to the fundamental unity of the language, which is hardly surprising in view of the centralizing power of the Empire itself and the strength of its traditions; but it was, in part at least, a first step toward further differential evolution.

It also seems that regional variations increased during the centuries that followed the end of the Empire, due to the new social, cultural, and indeed ethnic circumstances that arose within and between the new political units that broke the political unity of the Latin-speaking lands. We have already seen that as a result of the geographically varying nature of linguistic developments, the "death" of Latin as a living language may well have happened at different times in different places; the transformation of Latin into Romance and the split of Romance into separate Romance languages are thus closely related processes.

The reasons for the differentiation of Latin into different languages in different places are really the province of Romance historical linguists rather than of Vulgar Latinists; but it is also worth noting that here too there are not many uncontroversial details on which all the specialists agree. Research has been carried out since the late nineteenth century, for example, into the effects of the "substratum" languages (the languages already spoken in the different areas of the Empire at the time that the Romans settled there), but it has still not been shown conclusively that these had any effect at all on the territorial differentiation of Romance. A few decades later, particularly as a result of the work of the Swiss Romanist Walther von Wartburg (see the Bibliography), it became common to attribute the evolution of local variants of spoken Latin to the effect of the "superstratum" languages (the languages spoken by the peoples who settled in the area of the former Empire after its political demise), most obviously, of course, Germanic. Other locally relevant factors, such as the nature and chronology of the initial colonization and Romanization of an area, were certainly able to influence the later evolution of Latin. Even so, despite some promising initial ideas that have arisen from the examination and evaluation of these questions, no important extralinguistic factor seems yet to have been found to explain the differentiation.

3. The Main Lines of Vulgar Development

The evolution of Vulgar Latin represents the main line of the later development of Latin. Those aspects of Late Latin that are not "vulgar," such as the texts that essentially follow the traditionally prescribed forms of Latin, are of little interest to a linguist. Latin evolved in the form of Vulgar Latin, and that is where the interest of post-Classical Latin is to be found; and the Vulgar developments help us understand the way in which Romance began, as well as the future details of the Romance languages. So it is worthwhile summarizing here the main lines of this evolutionary process insofar as they can be glimpsed behind the mass of attestations, which when seen piecemeal can at times present a picture of a mere aggregation of unconnected details.

In phonetics, prosodic changes seem to have been decisive: the change in the nature of the accent; the loss of the phonological length system of the vowels, which was originally independent of the accent; followed by the reorganization of the vowel system. As regards the consonants, we can see the increasing effect of the phonetic context upon their realization, which led to the increasing growth of assimilatory tendencies; these are collectively the general conditions that led to a restructuring of the consonant system, to the enriched fricative subsystem, which had been relatively poor in Latin previously, and to the creation of a whole series of affricates unknown in Classical Latin. This reorganization was not completed, though, until the second half of the first millennium A.D.

In the grammatical system the main lines of development are particularly clear and very interesting. As regards morphology, we can see, as the Vulgar language develops, a progressive decrease in the number and the linguistic roles of paradigmatic features, accompanied by a concomitant increase in syntagmatic and distributional methods of conveying the same meaning; or, to portray the same process from a different perspective, the number of word inflections used decreases while the number and use of phrases composed of separate independent words increases.[4] The substitution of analytic for synthetic expressions went a long way in nominal morphology, progressing at different speeds in different areas, but in verbal morphology much less of a dent was made in the traditional synthetic ensemble of forms. This was, of course, a gradual evolutionary tendency, not an abrupt break. We could even add that the general view of the development of Latin into Romance as being a change from synthetic to analytic is no more than a convenient oversimplification that to some extent misrepresents what actually happened; for in Romance verbal morphology, especially, the grammar is still predominantly synthetic, and some of the analytic constructions that replaced the original synthetic forms have in time themselves become synthetic, with the result that Romance has new synthetic forms (the future and, most strikingly, the conditional, which Latin had never had before). So several synthetic paradigms, or parts of paradigms, are still there, despite the changes that occurred, such as the partial elimination of irregular and unusual inflectional patterns and the development of many regular forms to replace the initially irregular. Certainly, overall, we see a simplification in the formal systems that survive.

The changes just summarized are facts rather than value judgments, but it cannot be denied that they made the use of the language rather easier for its speakers. Juxtaposing invariant elements that do not change, that have a straightforward and relatively clear value, is a simpler way of expressing yourself, involving less concentration on detail and less chance of error than having perpetually to make choices, many times inside every single phrase, from a long list of complicated and varying inflections whose purpose was often ambiguous or unclear. The tendency to use regular forms rather than originally irregular synthetic forms was of course a step in this same general direction of requiring less effort from the speaker.

---

4. The varying inflected forms of a lexeme contain bound endings (or other variable features, such as the root vowel of a stem) that are fixed in an invariant position in the word and cannot be reordered; the words "synthetic" (for forms with such a bound inflection) and "analytic" (for combinations of separate words), which have been used freely in this book, are imprecise but useful metaphors.

We have seen several times that all these directions in which the language evolved were in a sense predictable, being traceable back to features of the original Latin structures such as the lack of symmetry between the different declensions, functional interferences between some of the nominal inflections, the equivalence in practice between some nominal inflections and prepositional phrases. These had been in the language all along, even in the most literary texts, which meant that from the start there already existed the potential for the decline in the use of nominal inflections and the substitution of analytical constructions for several oblique cases. The same thing can be said of other aspects of the traditional grammar. Even so, despite the fact that the evolution of the grammar of Late and Vulgar Latin was based on possibilities present in the language all along, the developments were not the result of internal factors alone. The development of the language toward the Romance structural type probably had its rate and scope determined by extralinguistic factors. We may need to take into account the massive entry into the Latin-language community of many people, including the many slaves imported into Italy itself, whose first language was something else. These had to learn the language as they went along, according to their local circumstances—that is, orally—since there was no institutionalized system for teaching them the language; and then maybe it was they who transmitted to their descendants the language that they had learned in this unsystematic way. This "foreigners' Latin" and also the Latin spoken by native-speakers who had extensive contact with speakers of another language—which initially meant most speakers in Italy and every speaker elsewhere—had necessarily a tendency to simplify the paradigms, to avoid the synthetic forms in favor of more manageable analytic alternatives; and it could have been this kind of Latin that took the lead in the evolution of Latin as a whole toward Romance, the "vulgar" evolution that we have seen outlined in this book. This is not the only external factor that is worth considering, but it is not hard to see that it probably had an important role to play here. But this is, in the end, only a hypothesis. The processes involved in the evolution of Vulgar Latin, in the development of late spoken Latin—in other words, in the entire development of Latin toward Romance—and the relationship and interference of internal and external factors in these changes are far from being clear even now; they have yet to be discovered and described with the necessary completeness and precision.

There is just room for a few final comments. We need to accept that the diachronic movement of Latin structures was not one single process in which the details were as interdependent as the cogs of a machine; changes in the different parts of the language seem usually to be unrelated, only affecting each other to a small extent, which means that we cannot often be clear about the causal relationship, if any, between separate phenomena. It seems clear now, for example, that the developments that occurred in the morphological system were not initiated—or were at the most only initiated in part—by phonetic or phonological changes. The same can be said about the relationship between the morphological and the syntactic changes; some changes in these two areas were undoubtedly connected, such as the simplification of the nominal inflectional system and the fixing of the word order within the noun phrase, but these innovations were not the result of a chain of cause and effect that only led in one direction. And it also needs to be stressed that the evolution that Latin underwent from a generally synthetic type of language toward a more analytic one, with the loss or regularization of complex inflectional paradigms, is not an inevitable and necessary direction for a language to evolve in. Evolutions in the other direction are entirely possible, and some synthetic languages have managed to remain synthetic for several millennia.

The study of Vulgar Latin ties in with the general study of historical linguistics in all these areas; the study of Vulgar Latin is an unusually well-documented example of linguistic change and has a crucial role to play therefore in more general research projects that are meant to illuminate the mechanisms and factors involved in language change and in the descriptions of the laws that govern the movement of languages in time.

Selective Bibliography

1. Textual Sources

Anthimi de observatione ciborum ad Theodoricum regem Francorum Epistula (*Corpus Medicorum Latinorum*, vol. 8.1). Edited by E. Liechtenhahn. Berlin: Teubner, 1963.

Antike Inschriften aus Jugoslavien. Edited by V. Hoffiller and B. Saria. Zagreb, 1938.

Antonini Placentini Itinerarium. In *Corpus Christianorum* 175, edited by Paul Geyer, 127–74. Brépols: Turnhout, 1965.

Apicius: L'art culinaire: De re coquinaria. Edited by Jacques André. Paris: Klincksieck, 1965.

The Book of Pontiffs (Liber Pontificalis) and *The Lives of the Eighth-Century Popes (Liber Pontificalis).* Translated by Raymond Davis. Liverpool: University of Liverpool Press, 1989/92.

Claudii Hermeri Mulomedicina Chironis. Edited by E. Oder. Leipzig: Teubner, 1901.

Codice Diplomatico Longobardo. Edited by L. Schiaparelli. Rome: Instituto Storico Italiano, 1929.

Corpus Inscriptionum Latinarum (CIL). 17 vols. Berlin: Reimer, 1863–.

Corpus Papyrorum Latinarum. Edited by Robert Cavenaile. Wiesbaden: Harrassowitz, 1958.

Defixionum tabellae quotquot innotuerunt tam in Graecis Orientis quam in totius Occidentis partibus. Edited by Auguste Audollent. Paris: Fontemoing, 1904. Reprint, Frankfurt: Minerva, 1967.

Die nichtliterarischen lateinischen Papyri Italiens aus der Zeit 445–700. 2 vols. Edited by J.O. Tjäder. Vol. I, Lund: Gleerup, 1954; vol. II, Stockholm: Svenska Institutet, 1982.

Egeria's Travels to the Holy Land. Translated by John Wilkinson. Jerusalem: Ariel, 1971. Revised ed., Warminster: Aris & Phillips, 1981.

Formulae Andecavenses, Formulae Merovingici et Karolini Aevi (MGH, *Legum Sectio* V). Edited by K. Zeumer. Hanover: Hahn, 1886.

Fredegarii et aliorum chronica (MGH, Scriptores rerum Merovingicarum, II). Edited by Bruno Krusch. Hanover: Hahn, 1888.

Grammatici Latini (GL). Vols. I–VII, edited by Heinrich Keil, Leipzig: Teubner, 1865–79. Vol. VIII, edited by H. Hagen, Leipzig: Teubner, 1923. All reprinted Hildesheim: Olms, 1981.

Grégoire de Tours, Histoire des Francs. 2 vols. Edited by Robert Latouche. Paris: Les Belles Lettres, 1975.

Gregorii Turonensis Opera: Pars I, Historia Francorum (MGH, Scriptores Rerum Merovingicarum, I.1). Edited by Wilhelm Arndt and Bruno Krusch. Hanover: Hahn, 1885.

Inscripciones cristianas de la España romana y visigoda. Edited by José Vives. 2d ed. Barcelona: CSIC, 1969.

Inscripciones romanas de Galicia. 4 vols. Edited by F. Bouza Brey et al. Santiago de Compostela: University of Santiago de Compostela, 1949–68.

Inscriptiones Christianae Italiae VII *Saec. Antiquiores (ICI)*. Bari: Edibuglia, 1985–.

Inscriptiones Christianae Urbis Romae Saec. VII *Antiquiores (ICVR)*. N.s. Rome/Vatican City, 1922–.

Inscriptiones Daciae et Scythiae Minoris antiquae. Edited by Dionis M. Pippidi and I. I. Russu. Bucharest: Rumanian Academy, 1975–83.

Inscriptiones Italiae. Rome: Libreria dello Stato, 1931–.

Inscriptiones Latinae Christianae Veteres (ILCV). 3 vols. Edited by E. Diehl. Berlin: Weidman, 1925–31. Revised vol. II, 1961.

Inscriptions de la Mésie Supérieure. Edited by Peter Petrovic and Fanoula Papazoglou. Belgrade: University of Belgrade, 1976–.

Inscriptions latines d'Algérie. Vol. I. Edited by Stéphane Gsell. Paris: Champion, 1922.

Inscriptions romaines de Catalogne. Edited by Georges Fabre, M. Mayer, and I. Rodà. Paris, 1984–87.

Itala: Das Neue Testament in altlateinischer Überlieferung. 4 vols. Edited by Adolf Jülicher, Walther Matzkow, and Kurt Aland. Berlin: De Gruyter, 1938–63.

Itinerarium Egeriae. In *Corpus Christianorum* 175, edited by Adriano Franceschini and R. Weber, 27–90. Brépols: Turnhout, 1965.

Le Liber Pontificalis: Texte, introduction et commentaire. 2 vols. Edited by Louis Duchesne. Paris: Bibliothèque des écoles Françaises d'Athènes et de Rome, 1886/92.

Lex Alamannorum (MGH, Legum Sectio I). Edited by K. Lehmann. Hanover: Hahn, 1888.

The Roman Inscriptions of Britain, I: Inscriptions on Stone. Edited by Robin G. Collingwood and Richard Wright. Oxford: Clarendon Press, 1965.

Tablettes Albertini: Actes privés de l'époque vandale. Edited by Christian Courtois et al. Paris: Arts et Métiers Graphiques, 1952.

Theodosii De Situ Terrae Sanctae. In *Corpus Christianorum* 175, edited by P. Geyer, 114–25. Brépols: Turnhout, 1965.

Vetus Latina: Die Reste der altlateinischen Bibel. Edited by Bonifatius Fischer. Freiburg: Herder, 1949–.

Vindolanda: The Latin Writing Tablets. 2 vols. Edited by Alan K. Bowman and J. David Thomas. London: Britannia Monographs, 1983/94.

2. Studies

Adams, J. N. *Pelagonius and Latin Veterinary Terminology in the Roman Empire.* Leiden: Brill, 1995.

———. "Some Neglected Evidence for Latin *Habeo* with Infinitive: The Order of the Constituents." *Transactions of the Philological Society* 89 (1991): 131–96.

———. "A Typological Approach to Latin Word Order." *Indogermanische Forschungen* 81 (1976): 27–59.

———. *The Vulgar Latin of the Letters of Claudius Terentianus.* Manchester: University of Manchester Press, 1977.

Allen, W. Sidney. *Vox Latina.* Cambridge: Cambridge University Press, 1970.

Aufstieg und Niedergang der römischen Welt [ANRW], II: Kaiserzeit. Vols. 29.1 and 29.2. Edited by Wolfgang Haase and Hildegard Temporim. Berlin: De Gruyter, 1983.

Banniard, Michel. *Du Latin aux langues romanes.* Paris: Nathan, 1997.

———. *Viva Voce: Communication écrite et communication orale du VIe au IXe siècle en Occident latin.* Paris: Études Augustiniennes, 1992.

Beckmann, G. A. *Die Nachfolgekonstruktionen des instrumentalen Ablativs im Spätlatein und im Französischen* (Zeitschrift für Romanische Philologie, Beiheft 106). Tübingen: Niemeyer, 1963.

Bonnet, Max. *Le latin de Grégoire de Tours.* Paris: Hachette, 1890.

Calboli, Gualtiero. *Über das Lateinische: Vom Indogermanischen zu dem romanischen Sprachen.* Tübingen: Niemeyer, 1997.

———, ed. *Latin vulgaire, latin tardif II: Actes du IIe Colloque international sur le latin vulgaire et tardif.* Tübingen: Niemeyer, 1990.

Callebat, Louis, ed. *Latin vulgaire–latin tardif IV: Actes du IVe Colloque international sur le latin vulgaire et tardif.* Hildesheim: Olms-Weidmann, 1995.

Carnoy, A. *Le latin d'Espagne d'après les inscriptions: Étude linguistique.* 2d ed. Louvain: Istas, 1906.

Coseriu, Eugenio. *El llamado latín vulgar y las primeras diferenciaciones romances.* Montevideo: University of Montevideo, 1954.

Dahmen, Wolfgang, et al. *Latein und Romanisch.* Tübingen: Narr, 1987.

Díaz y Díaz, Manuel C. *Antología del latín vulgar.* Madrid: Gredos, 1974.

Diez, Friedrich. *Grammatik der romanischen Sprachen.* 2 vols. Bonn: Weber, 1836–43.

Du Cange [Charles Du Fresne, Sieur Du Cange]. *Glossarium Mediae et Infimae Latinitatis.* 10 vols. London: Niort, 1884–87. Reprint, Paris, 1954.

Ettmayer, K. von. "Vulgärlatein." In *Geschichte der indogermanischen Sprachwissenschaft seit ihrer Begründung durch Fr. Bopp,* edited by Wilhelm Streitberg, II.1:231–80. Strasbourg: Trubner, 1916.

Gaeng, Paul A. *The Collapse and Reorganization of Latin Nominal Inflection.* Potomac, Md.: Scripta Humanistica, 1984.

———. *An Inquiry into Local Variations in Vulgar Latin As Reflected in the Vocalism of Christian Inscriptions.* Chapel Hill: University of North Carolina Press, 1968.

———. *A Study of Nominal Inflection in Latin Inscriptions: A Morphosyntactic Analysis.* Chapel Hill: University of North Carolina Press, 1977.

García Ruiz, E. "Estudio lingüístico de las *defixiones* latinas no incluidas en el Corpus de Audollent." *Emerita* 35 (1967): 55–89, 219–48.

Goelzer, Henri. *Étude lexicographique et grammaticale de la latinité de Saint-Jérome.* Paris: Hachette, 1884.

Grandgent, C. H. *An Introduction to Vulgar Latin.* London: Heath, 1907.

Harris, Martin B., and Nigel Vincent, eds. *The Romance Languages.* London: Croom Helm, 1988.

Haudricourt, André G., and Alphonse G. Juilland. *Essai pour une histoire structurale du phonétisme français.* Paris: Klincksieck, 1943.

Herman, József. *Du latin aux langues romanes: Études de linguistique historique.* Tübingen: Niemeyer, 1990.

———. "L'état actuel des recherches sur le latin vulgaire et tardif." *Studia Romanica (Societas Japonica Studiorum Romanicorum)* 28 (1995): 1–18.

———. *La formation du système roman des conjonctions de subordination.* Berlin: Akademie, 1963.

———. "La situation linguistique en Italie au VIe siècle." *Revue de Linguistique Romane* 52 (1988): 285–302.

———, ed. "La fragmentation linguistique de la Romania." In *Actes du XXe Congrès de Linguistique et Philologie Romanes*, II:645–98. Tübingen: Francke, 1993.

———, ed. *Latin vulgaire, latin tardif: Actes du Ier Colloque international sur le latin vulgaire et tardif.* Tübingen: Niemeyer, 1987.

———, ed. *La transizione dal latino alle lingue romanze.* Tübingen: Niemeyer, 1998.

Hofmann, Johann B., and Anton Szantyr. *Lateinische Grammatik.* Vol. II, *Lateinische Syntax und Stilistik.* Munich: Beck, 1965.

Iliescu, Maria, and Werner Marxgut, eds. *Latin vulgaire, latin tardif III: Actes du IIIe Colloque international sur le latin vulgaire et tardif.* Tübingen: Niemeyer, 1992.

Iliescu, Maria, and Dan Slusanski. *Du latin aux langues romanes: Choix de textes traduits et commentés du IIe siècle avant J.C. jusqu'au Xe siècle après J.C.* Wilhelmsfeld: Egert, 1991.

Jeanneret, M. *La langue des tablettes d'exécration latines.* Diss., Neuchâtel, 1916.

Kiss, Sandor. *Tendances évolutives de la syntaxe verbale en latin tardif.* Debrecen: University, 1982.

———. *Les transformations de la structure syllabique en latin tardif.* Debrecen: University, 1972.

Kramer, Johannes. *Literarische Quellen zur Aussprache des Vulgärlateins.* Meisenheim: Hain, 1976.

Lloyd, Paul M. *From Latin to Spanish: Vol. I.* Philadelphia: American Philosophical Society, 1987.

———. "On the Definition of Vulgar Latin." *Neuphilologische Mitteilungen* 80 (1979): 110–22.
Löfstedt, Bengt. "Rückschau und Ausblick auf die vulgärlateinische Forschung: Quellen und Methoden." In *Aufstieg und Niedergang der römischen Welt*, II, 29.1:453–79.
———. *Studien über die Sprache der langobardischen Gesetze: Quellen und Methoden.* Uppsala: Almqvist & Wiksell, 1961.
Löfstedt, Einar. *Late Latin.* Oslo: Aschehoug, 1959.
———. *Syntactica: Studien und Beiträge zur historischen Syntax des Lateins.* 2 vols. Lund: Gleerup, 1942.
Lot, Ferdinand. "A quelle époque a-t-on cessé de parler latin?" *Bulletin du Cange* (= *Archivum Latinitatis Medii Aevi*) 6 (1931): 97–159.
Lüdtke, Helmut. *Die strukturelle Entwicklung des romanischen Vokalismus.* Bonn: Romanische Seminar, 1956.
Meyer-Lübke, Wilhelm. *Grammaire des langues romanes.* 4 vols. Paris: Welter, 1890–1906.
Mihăescu, H. *La langue latine dans le sud-est de l'Europe.* Paris: Les Belles Lettres, 1978. Rumanian original, Bucharest: Academy, 1960.
Mohrmann, Christine. *Études sur le latin des chrétiens.* 4 vols. Rome: Edizioni di Storia e Letteratura, 1958–77.
Muller, Henri F. *A Chronology of Vulgar Latin.* Tübingen: Niemeyer, 1929.
Muller, Henri F., and Pauline Taylor. *A Chrestomathy of Vulgar Latin.* Boston: Heath, 1932.
Neumann, G., and J. Untermann. *Die Sprachen im Römischen Reich der Kaiserzeit* (*Bonner Jahrbücher*, Beiheft 80). Cologne-Bonn: Rheinland, 1980.
Norberg, Dag. *Beiträge zur spätlateinischen Syntax.* Uppsala: Almqvist & Wiksell, 1944.
Omeltchenko, S. W. *A Quantitative and Comparative Study of the Vocalism of the Latin Inscriptions of North Africa, Britain, Dalmatia, and the Balkans.* Chapel Hill: University of North Carolina Press, 1977.
Panhuis, Dirk G. *The Communicative Perspective in the Sentence: A Study of Latin Word Order.* Amsterdam: Benjamins, 1982.
Pei, Mario A. *The Language of the Eighth-Century Texts in Northern France.* New York: Carranza, 1932.
Petersmann, Hubert, ed. *Latin vulgaire–latin tardif V: Actes du Ve Colloque international sur le latin vulgaire et tardif.* Heidelberg: Winter, 1999.
Pinkster, Harm. *Latin Syntax and Semantics.* London: Routledge, 1990.
Pirson, J. *La langue des inscriptions latines de la Gaule.* Brussels: Société Belge de Librairie, 1901.
Schuchardt, Hugo. *Der Vokalismus des Vulgärlateins.* 3 vols. Leipzig: Teubner, 1866–68.
Selig, Maria. *Die Entwicklung der Nominaldeterminanten in Spätlatein.* Tübingen: Narr, 1992.
Solin, Heikki, Olli Salomies, and Uta-Maria Liertz, eds. *Acta Colloquii Epigraphici Latini Helsingiae.* Helsinki: Societas Scientiarum Fennica, 1995.

Souter, Alexander. *A Glossary of Later Latin to 600 A.D.* Oxford: Clarendon Press, 1949.
Straka, Georges. "Observations sur la chronologie et les dates de quelques modifications phonétiques en roman et en français prélitteraire." *Revue des Langues Romanes* 71 (1953): 247–307.
Svennung, J. *Untersuchungen zu Palladius und zur lateinischen Fach- und Volkssprache.* Uppsala: Almqvist & Wiksell, 1935.
Thesaurus Linguae Latinae. Leipzig: Teubner, 1900–. [Now at the letter *P*.]
Tovar, Antonio. "A Research Report on Vulgar Latin and Its Local Variations." *Kratylos* 9 (1964): 113–34.
Väänänen, Veikko. *Étude sur le texte et la langue des Tablettes Albertini.* Helsinki, 1965.
———. *Introduction au latin vulgaire.* Paris: Klincksieck, 1963.
———. *Le journal-épître d'Egerie (Itinerarium Egeriae): Étude linguistique.* Helsinki: Societas Scientiarum Fennica, 1987.
———. *Le latin vulgaire des inscriptions pompéiennes.* Helsinki: Société de Littérature Finnoise, 1937. New edition, Berlin: Akademie, 1966.
———. "Le problème de la diversification du latin." In *Aufstieg und Niedergang der römischen Welt,* II, 29.1:480–506.
van Uytfanghe, Marc. "Le latin des hagiographes mérovingiens et la protohistoire du français." *Romanica Gandensia* 16 (1976): 5–89.
———. "Histoire du latin, protohistoire des langues romanes et histoire de la communication." *Francia* 11 (1984): 579–613.
Varvaro, Alberto. *Storia, problemi e metodi della linguistica romanza.* Naples: Liguori, 1968.
Velázquez Soriano, Isabel. *Las pizarras visigodas: Edición crítica y estudio.* Murcia: University of Murcia, 1989.
Wanner, Dieter. *The Development of Romance Clitic Pronouns: From Latin to Old Romance.* Berlin: De Gruyter, 1987.
Wartburg, Walther von. *La fragmentation linguistique de la Romania.* Paris: Klincksieck, 1967.
Weinrich, Harald. *Phonologische Studien zur romanischen Sprachgeschichte.* Münster: Aschendorff, 1958.
Wright, Roger. *Early Ibero-Romance.* Newark, Del.: Juan de la Cuesta, 1995.
———. *Late Latin and Early Romance in Spain and Carolingian France.* Liverpool: Francis Cairns, 1982.
———. "Latin in Spain: Early Ibero-Romance." In *The Origins and Development of Emigrant Languages,* edited by Hans F. Nielsen and Lene Schøsler, 277–98. Odense: University of Odense, 1996.
———, ed. *Latin and the Romance Languages in the Early Middle Ages.* London: Routledge, 1991. Reprint, University Park: Pennsylvania State University Press, 1996.
Zamboni, Alberto. "Dal latino tardo agli albori romanzi: Dinamiche linguistiche della transizione." In *Morfologie sociali e culturali in Europa fra tarda antichità e alto medioevo,* 619–702. Spoleto, 1998.

Printed in Great Britain
by Amazon